Who's My Da

A Tale of DNA
Surprises and Discovery

© Joel Gottfried
2021

Contents

Chapter 1 The Question Arises 1

Chapter 2 What Does This Even Mean? 11

Chapter 3 My Social Father 16

Chapter 4 The Search Begins..28

Chapter 5 That's Not All 34

Chapter 6 How Do You Even Spell DNA? 41

Chapter 7 First Contact 47

Chapter 8 What About The Doctor?...50

Chapter 9 Barking Up Some Family Trees 56

Chapter 10 Maimoona 61

Chapter 11 More Connections..64

Chapter 12 The Levines 68

Chapter 13 Dawn Bhat...75

Chapter 14 David Levine Again 80

Chapter 15 The Big Reveal 87

Chapter 16 My New Family..90

Chapter 17 My Biological Father..99

Chapter 18 What Really Happened? 108

Chapter 19 What Now?..116

Acknowledgments..123

Chapter 1

The Question Arises

I have always been fascinated by history and especially by personal history. A number of years ago I decided to follow up on this interest by learning about and then utilizing the tools of genealogy to find as much as I could about my ancestors. While other family members in varying degrees share my interest, I am without doubt the family genealogist. There are a seemingly infinite number of details to unearth. And the more I find the more interesting it becomes. I like the problem-solving detective work that it entails. But even more so I love learning about the people I come from. There is a romantic allure of what their lives were like so long ago.

I started thinking about this seriously back in 2005. I attended seminars and learned about sources and methods. The first step was to build a family tree with my immediate family (mom, dad, my younger siblings Debbie and Stuart, and both sets of grandparents). I would then decide which ancestral path to follow first. When doing this type of research you have four paths to choose from. One for each of your four grandparents.

By the time I began my research neither my dad nor any of my grandparents were still alive. So I started by interviewing my mom to get information about her side of the family. Her recollections and record-keeping were somewhat limited so I was off to a slow start. I did find some information about her uncle Julius (for whom I am named) but didn't have much else to go on.

Even though I couldn't talk to my dad, he was definitively a much more valuable source of information. Throughout his life, he had been a very careful record keeper. When I went through his papers I found a treasure trove of documents and artifacts that could seed my search.

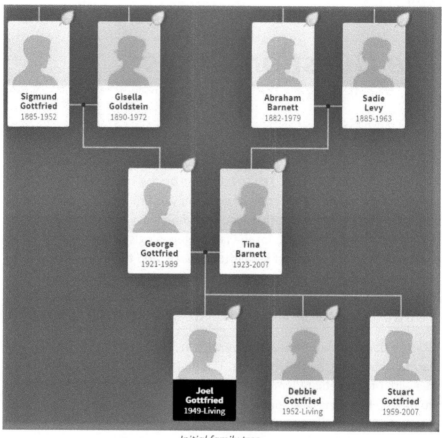

Initial family tree

His parents, Gizella and Sigmund Gottfried were persecuted European Jews who had fled the hardships and anti-Semitism of Hungary. They had boarded steamships with lower-class accommodations and endured the difficult transatlantic journey to reach the promised land of the United States. But to us grandkids, they were just Grandma Gussie (not sure why this was better or more Americanized than Gizella) and Grandpa Jimmy (I have absolutely no idea where this came from).

They didn't know each other in Hungary and came across in separate ships around the turn of the 20th century. My grandfather was 19 and traveled with a couple of relatives. My grandmother was 16, the oldest of five children, and traveled with her whole family. In each instance, they sailed right up to Ellis Island and debarked literally in the shadow of the Statue of Liberty. I have copies of the ship manifests that show them as passengers. I can see the handwritten entries from the immigration agents at Ellis Island describing their origins, appearance, other family members, and even how much money they had with them. Fascinating stuff to me.

After these initial findings, I thought that the easiest way forward would be to continue my research with Grandma Gussie's family. Besides the availability of documents and some living cousins of hers, I had a real fondness for her. I simply wanted to know more about her 'back story'.

She was a sweet woman who had endured so much in her life but still was able to share warmth and love with her grandchildren. She had no pretenses. What you saw was what you got. And what you saw, was just what you would expect a Jewish grandmother to look like. A friendly face topped with wavy gray hair on top of a short, stocky body. I never saw her wear anything other than plain and matronly-looking dresses. Her apartment always smelled great with the scents of classic Hungarian food in the air. Through her heavily accented English, she had no problem sharing her affection.

One of my very earliest memories of any kind was of an incident with Grandma Gussie. I was barely 4 years old and my dad had brought me to her small apartment in the Bronx for a visit and a sleepover. I think this was my very first sleepover anywhere but home. We were living in Queens by then so this was a bit of a journey. I don't remember the details of the early part of the evening. But I vividly recall waking up in the middle of the night and freaking out about my unfamiliar surroundings. I was crying and screaming and completely inconsolable. My dad had to make a second round trip from Queens to come and get me. The most memorable part of the evening however was Grandma's reaction to all this. As my dad carried me out on his shoulder I was looking backward into the apartment. My grandma was completely distraught. She was crying and heaving and repeatedly blowing her nose. Her reaction was so powerful that it brought me up short. I clearly remember stopping my wailing to take notice of her distress.

Through the years she didn't seem to me to have an unusual number of colds or other respiratory illnesses. However, she always had a pack of Pine Brothers cherry cough drops in her purse. My sister Debbie and I called them 'Specials' and treated these like candy. No visit to Grandma Gussie's was complete without at least one 'Special' each.

Grandma Gussie with Debbie and me at Grandpa Jimmy's grave, 1957

When grandma was getting on in years, she began experiencing early signs of dementia. To keep a closer eye on her my dad moved her to a basement apartment in a house not too far from ours. He and I would visit her every Sunday afternoon to make sure she was OK. Besides the joy of seeing her, smelling and tasting the food and the 'Specials' these visits were particularly rewarding for me. Due to her creeping dementia, she had lost the ability to make and count change. So every purchase she made was only with bills. Any coins that were part of the transaction were just dropped into her purse, never to be seen again. By the end of the week, it was a marvel that she could even carry this overladen purse out the front door. For me, however, this was a gold mine! My dad would give her money for the week ahead and I would get to empty and keep all of the coins.

Against this backdrop, for my 69th birthday in March of 2018, my sister Debbie gave me a DNA kit from the popular company 23andMe. By using my DNA results we hoped that I might find living relatives who would share the same ancestors I was trying to research. This had the potential to accelerate my search and ultimately expand the contours of my current family.

As part of the present, she also bought a DNA kit for herself. As brother and sister, we clearly would have identical genealogical ancestors. But through the vagaries of DNA transmission and recombination, we might get different clues as to who these common ancestors might be. And besides, it would be fun to share results and do this together. My brother, Stuart, had died in 2007 so he, unfortunately, couldn't be included in our DNA journey. The tests, we knew, could also provide information about potentially worrisome health markers in our DNA. My family often complains that I am a hard person to get a present for. This was a dramatic exception to that problem.

My results came in first and I didn't have any markers for Alzheimer's or Parkinson's or any other inheritable diseases that they track. The results indicated that I was 98% Ashkenazi Jewish and descended primarily from people in Eastern Europe. Nothing surprising there. When I went to look for DNA relatives I found a handful of 2nd cousins and lots and lots of more distant relatives. Though I was initially so excited to do this I wasn't sure at first what to do with these results.

Then on May 25th, Debbie gave me a call to let me know that her results had also posted on the 23andMe site. She was having some issues accessing and interpreting the results. So she told me her password and I logged in as her to get the process started. I did all this while she was still on the phone. After making the appropriate sharing settings so we could see each other's results she magically appeared at the top of my list as my closest relative. And I was at the top of hers.

What happened next was utterly unexpected. According to the 23andMe analysis, we were only half-siblings, not full siblings. To say I was stunned is an understatement. How could this be? It made no sense. Of course, we were brother and sister. We had lived our entire lives as brother and sister. There must be some kind of mistake.

There are times in your life when something dramatic and important happens. You receive some bad news that was unexpected or perhaps finally hear the results of something you were dreading. Typically in these cases, your body is awash with emotions to accompany the cognition of the event. This has certainly been my experience. Maybe you begin sweating, or your pulse quickens, or you become short of breath, or your stomach is in knots etc. Not in this case. This was such a bizarre turn of events that I didn't absorb what was happening. My mind was confused and my body remained unchanged. I wasn't suppressing my feelings. I just didn't have any. This wasn't unwelcome news, it wasn't news at all. It was simply some bizarre error that had no impact on me.

When I took a more detailed look at the results I saw why they claimed we were only half-siblings. Full siblings will, on average, share 50% of their DNA. DNA is found on 22 pairs of chromosomes (the 23rd chromosome is the sex chromosome). One strand in each pair is from the mother and the other from the father. Not only would full siblings expect to find an approximately 50% match, but they would expect about half of their matches to come from 'Fully Identical Regions' that match on both the maternal and paternal strands.

Debbie and I shared a bit less than 27% of our DNA. The average amount that half-siblings would share would be 25%. Just as telling as the smaller amount of shared DNA is the fact that there were no Fully Identical Regions. These results were a textbook case of half-siblings.

Since we knew with a great degree of certainty that we had the same mother, the question I asked Debbie was, "So who is your daddy?" Her instantaneous reply to me was, "Who is **your** daddy?" Interestingly, the immediate thinking of each of us was that of course, our father was our father. As we tried to process this Debbie gave me some rather persuasive anecdotal evidence to support her position that I was the one with a different father.

My mom and dad, Tina Barnett and George Gottfried were married quite young. She was barely 21 and he was 23. They were eager to have children and despite some time apart due to the war, they set about trying to create a family. By 1948, the year I was ultimately conceived as their first born they had been married over five years and had not had any success in their family goals. So by then, the frustration of many years of failing to conceive might have convinced one or both of them to try something different.

Mom and dad wedding day 1943

In addition to this, there was no question that I didn't look like my father. I have neither the body type nor the facial features of a Gottfried. Growing up I was always considered to be more of a Barnett. Debbie on the other hand was a Gottfried through and through. And our younger brother Stuart was 'George junior'.

While the anecdotal evidence indicated it was me who needed to go searching, I still couldn't believe it. It just didn't feel true. There was absolutely nothing in the way that either of my parents interacted with me to suggest that I was anything other than their first and full child.

So far, no concerns about my ancestry

I contacted 23andMe technical support to see what the chances of an error just like this might be. By 'just like this' I mean correctly identifying half of the DNA matches that indicated we were at least half-siblings but somehow missing the remaining half that would have shown we were full siblings. Before I contacted them I knew this was extraordinarily unlikely. And by 'extraordinarily unlikely' I really meant 'impossible'. Nonetheless, I pursued my line of inquiry with them. I can be a dogged and precise (some would say persnickety) questioner. Although I asked very specific questions they refused to give me equally specific answers. Who could really blame them? I was asking them to speculate and quantify situations that just didn't occur. But I was desperate. Despite the implications of the data (which I normally revered) I just didn't believe this could be true. It just couldn't. With each email interchange, my questions became more and more pointed and their replies became less and less responsive. By the fourth attempt to get this very specific question answered they not only failed to address my concerns but became downright belligerent.

There was overwhelming evidence that we were only half-siblings, but the anecdotal evidence that it was me with a different father, while suggestive, was far from conclusive. With technical support of no help, Debbie and I figured out a different way to determine for sure who was George's child and who wasn't.

We have a cousin, Roy, who we had lost touch with. He is our dad's brother's son. If we could find him and convince him to take a DNA test then that would settle it. Without too much trouble Debbie found him and explained the predicament we were in. He said he would be happy to help out. So we sent him a 23andMe DNA kit and eagerly awaited the results. While we were waiting I kept thinking about what all this meant. I was sure his DNA analysis would put a lie to the crazy results we already had. That is, it would show that he was, as he always had been, a first cousin to both of us. I could then triumphantly return to 23andMe technical support with my middle finger raised high and a giant 'I told you so' on my lips. When his DNA results came back a few weeks later they were crystal clear. They conclusively showed he is Debbie's first cousin and he is not related to me.

This made me update my family tree and realize that the question was mine and mine alone.

"Who's my daddy?"

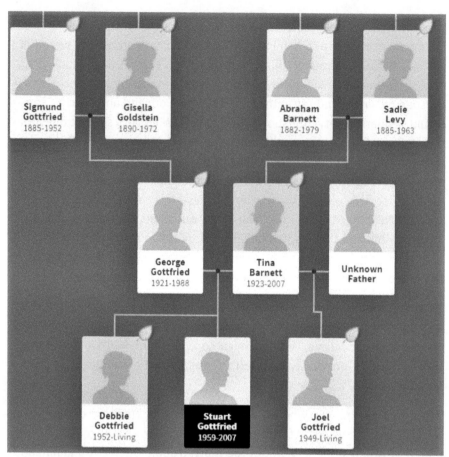

Updated family tree

Chapter 2

What Does This Even Mean?

When we first saw the DNA results, both Debbie and I were stunned. We could have been on the phone all day trying to make sense of this. As luck would have it I had to abruptly end my call with her after about 30 minutes because I had an appointment with my therapist. What perfect timing!

I have been seeing the same therapist off and on for 30 years. During this time she has helped me navigate my life through numerous issues. Some of them are mundane here-and-now types of dilemmas while others are long-simmering personality traits stemming from childhood experiences. She was with me during divorce, life-threatening illness, and the tolls of aging. I have poured my heart out to her and shared my deepest vulnerabilities. No one in the world knows me as thoroughly and deeply as she does. There certainly was no one else better suited to help me make sense of this shocking development.

When I got to her office I told her that I wanted to postpone the discussion we had been having for the past few weeks for something brand new. I pointed out that if she looked closely at my body she would see the scrolling chyron that blared 'BREAKING NEWS'. I related what had just happened with the emphasis on 'just'. Interestingly we did not delve deeply into the meaning of it all. We didn't tackle questions like: What did it feel like to have your world upended? What did it feel like to have your father snatched from you as a 69-year-old? What did it feel like to be a partial outsider in your own family? What did it feel like not to know where you came from? Or, most basically, what did it feel like?

Needless to say, we spoke about my feelings all the time. That was what therapy was all about. But in this session I simply told her the facts and that it was my opinion that when all was said and done this would prove to be, in the vernacular of the day, 'fake news'. I laughed about how this was just another crazy event in my life that would prove to be nothing more than a good story to tell. I just did not believe it. It was too preposterous to be true. I wasn't in denial so much as I was in disbelief.

Even after the 23andMe tech support fiasco I still didn't feel like this was my new reality. When the results from our cousin Roy arrived however I was finally jolted into admitting that a fundamental part of my identity was different than what I had always assumed. In fact, 'assumed' is way too strong a word. Who 'assumes' that their parents are in fact their real parents. It is just baked so deep into your reality that it never rises even close to your consciousness.

My discovery with Debbie was on the Friday right before Memorial Day Weekend. I had contacted 23andMe technical support that same day and their initial reply was that one of their DNA experts would examine my case right after the holiday weekend. This was fair enough. In the meantime, I wasn't sure how to proceed.

I quickly decided that one way to process this unexpected, unnerving and unwelcome news was to talk about it. So I mentioned this to friends and relatives. Perhaps in the telling and retelling of the story, it would all make more sense to me. And perhaps the inevitable questions and observations I would receive from others might also help me focus my attention on areas I hadn't thought about. In the early days of this process, I was convinced (against the available information) that this was somehow a mistake. So at the very least, this would be an entertaining story.

Although I thought this would indeed be an interesting story to tell I didn't expect the universal fascination with it that I received. Of course, both of my adult sons, with families of their own, were not only amazed to hear about all this but had a personal stake in the outcome. For them, the question was "Who is my Grandpa?" While my dad died young at age 67, they both knew him and had distinct memories of his larger-than-life persona.

My friends, while having no personal stake in the results, were equally intrigued. My wife, Susan, and I had an impromptu dinner with our close friends Lisa and Joel the night of my discovery. And after ordering our food and sharing the normal pleasantries of the day, I told them what had transpired earlier in the day. Joel's first thought summed up the reaction I had from so many. He said, "And you waited 10 minutes to tell us this!" Lisa is a doctor and I asked her how strong her knowledge of genetics is. Although she knew a fair amount she volunteered to send the 23andMe results from Debbie and me to a colleague of hers who specializes in this. Now we were getting somewhere.

The other thing that kept happening was a bit unexpected. Not only was there universal interest and fascination with my story, but I kept finding out that I wasn't alone. While none of my friends had even a remotely similar tale of their own, it seemed that every one of them knew people who did. Or had heard of people who did. Or had just read a magazine article about people who did. If my friends were a representative sample of the population (which by the way they are most definitely not!) there seemed to be an epidemic of surprising DNA testing run amok.

Another question that I always got was whether I felt that I was different or didn't belong in my family as I was growing up. My basic answer is 'no'. I was treated (and mistreated) no differently than my siblings. However, I was different in a couple of ways that now make more sense to me. I was significantly taller than everyone else. When I stopped growing as a 16-year old I topped out as a 6' 2" string bean. While my parents weren't unusually short this was notable. I was the tallest person in both my immediate and extended families. My father would always refer to me as 'stretch'.

The other difference was more telling. I was an academic whiz kid in school. I was always in the top class and even then found the work quite easy. I was especially good at math and science. And it wasn't just mastering schoolwork. I naturally saw the world through an analytic lens that always had me digging for greater understanding and first principles. To say that this stood out from the rest of my family was a dramatic understatement. My mom was advised to skip academics in high school and instead was steered into the 'commercial track'. My dad, because of the need to work, didn't focus much on school and had indifferent results. And neither of my siblings experienced anywhere near the same academic successes I had.

But where did this leave me? After the results from cousin Roy came in there was no longer any plausible deniability of my new reality. I had to wrestle with the fact that I did indeed have a different life story to tell.

I had taken to jokingly correcting anyone who referenced my sister to use 'half-sister'. I even began calling her my 'childhood acquaintance'. But these jokes completely belied what was actually happening with us. She called to check in with me every single day. Ironically after finding out we were more distant biological relatives than we thought we became even closer actual relatives. She was particularly good at adding context to many of my and our childhood memories. Although she is three years younger than me she was way more observant about what life in our family was all about. She was also remarkably good at pulling the levers of modern-day social media tools to search for our parents' contemporaries. With some ingenuity and good luck, she wound up finding our father's still living 97-year-old best friend and our aunt's sister. And she set out to talk to them and see what they might know. More than just these actions was my sense that she saw this as a joint venture. We were in this together. It is hard to over-emphasize how comforting this was.

March 1953

Debbie getting the ride of her life

In subsequent therapy sessions, I did delve into the deeper meaning of my discovery. Who am I? Nature vs. nurture. Just what and who is a 'father'. The primary definition for the verb 'to mother' is 'bring up a child with care and affection'. 'To father', in contrast, means little more than 'impregnate'. What about my father? And for that matter, what about me as a father? These were all questions that we examined and re-examined over the next few months.

Chapter 3

My Social Father

In every sense save one, George was my father. He raised me, loved me, provided for me, and mightily influenced my outlook on the world. In some cases, my worldview was in direct opposition to his. But it was undisputedly shaped by this man.

I have learned that this phenomenon is now common enough that there is a term for 'the father who raised you'. He is referred to as your 'social father' as opposed to your 'biological father'. What parts of who I am come from the decades of exposure to my social father vs. the potent power of my biological father's DNA? This is of course the classic, nature vs. nurture debate. But how did it play out for me? Until I found out who my biological father was I couldn't even begin to make that comparison. But it didn't stop me from thinking more about who my dad was as a man, a husband, and a father and what this meant for me. So who was my social father?

He was born in 1921 as the youngest of three sons. He had twin older brothers Armand and Harold. His dad died when I was three and just a few days after Debbie was born. So our knowledge of my dad's father is only through stories, pictures, and documents. From all accounts, the lives of the Gottfried family as Jewish immigrants in New York City were very difficult. In addition to all the issues facing immigrants at that time, they had to survive ill health and of course the great depression. His dad had been trained as a machinist and had a marketable skill but was often too ill to work. He ultimately succumbed to his illnesses and died at the age of 67. As was the custom in those days my dad's mom had no formal job training. She wound up working in sweat shops for minimal pay and then for the minimum wage of 25 cents an hour when it was introduced in 1938. Maintaining a family of five with this income was virtually impossible. All the sons were expected to earn money to help out. It was the only way to survive those harsh times. Living like this had a profound effect on my father. He valued hard work, the importance of having money, and having respect for the poor and disadvantaged.

The Gottfried clan circa 1930. Dad's twin brothers Harold and Armand standing with Grandpa Jimmy. Grandma Gussie and dad in the front.

These traits had their ups and downs for being a father to three children. The most obvious downside was the sheer amount of time and energy and attention he put into his work. This was clearly at the expense of time with his family. He worked six long days a week and then caught up on his paperwork on Sundays. He was a salesman, so the extra time and attention usually had a direct impact on his earnings.

By the time I was a teenager I had to be creative just to see him. In those days, New York had many daily newspapers. I picked up the Times on my way to school and we had the afternoon Long Island Star Journal delivered to our house. During his day, my dad picked up the Herald Tribune and the Post. Occasionally one of us would add the Journal American to our collection. Even though I already had had dinner with my mom and siblings at a normal dinner hour, I made it a point to join my dad for his dinner when he got home. This was typically about nine PM. We swapped newspapers and consumed both the news of the day and the food of the day (for me a second round of food). It is little wonder that I have a lifetime appetite for news and late-night snacking.

Dad and me circa 1960

Most of the time we spent at the dinner table was silent. We read and we ate and only occasionally shared our thoughts about the day's events. Nonetheless, it was a time of genuine connection. At this point you might be asking, "Who in their right mind would read five newspapers a day?" After getting the news from one of them, the others were being read primarily for their opinion columns. New York had many great columnists who offered different and thought-provoking insights into what was going on in the world. Fast forward to today and the way I consume news in this vastly different media landscape bears a striking resemblance to those dinner table rendezvous with my dad. Today my primary means of understanding the world around me is through a carefully curated set of people I follow on Twitter. Though my politics would definitely be called 'progressive' I also follow a fair number of conservative commentators and feel I have a richer understanding of the world by having to wrestle with their takes on the issues. To this date, I have not been able to find a single clear-eyed, honest, and insightful conservative commentator who supports Donald Trump. Does one even exist? Can one even exist?

One Saturday around Christmas time when I was 13 or 14 I accompanied my dad to work. This typically just involved sitting in his car that was illegally parked in Manhattan while he serviced one of his accounts. On this particular day, he found a legal spot so I joined him with his client. As we were walking down the street I pointed to one of the ubiquitous vendors who were selling chestnuts that they were roasting on their charcoal hibachis. I said, "Look at that. What a gyp. 25 cents and all you get is a few chestnuts." His reaction was swift and visceral. He grabbed me by my jacket and literally lifted me off the ground. He proceeded to lecture me about the sanctity of hard work and the need to be charitable to these men who were trying to support their families in the only way that they could. This event has had a profound and lasting effect on me. To this day I have a deeply felt empathy for those less well off than I am and an abiding respect for their hard work.

His reverence for money was truly extreme. After he retired, he and my mom and little brother Stuart all moved to Florida, near Ft. Lauderdale. Linda, my first wife, and I would typically visit around Christmas time. Back in those days we were both educators and had time off during the holiday season. On our visit in 1977, we had potentially very big news. We had been trying to have a child and we thought that she might be pregnant. For this visit, we had planned on visiting Key West. On the way to Key West, we stopped at a clinic in Miami to get a pregnancy test. On the way back from Key West we picked up the results. We were thrilled that it was indeed positive. Our little David was on his way. When we got back to my parents' house we broke the good news. My dad's response was unforgettable. He spent the entire evening silent and sullen. Not a single word of congratulations or joy, upon hearing the news of his first grandchild. Why? Because Linda and I were teachers and in his mind weren't wealthy enough to adequately provide for a child.

After the war and discharge from the Army, my dad trained to be a furrier with his uncle's business. By all accounts, he was quite skilled and definitely hard working. However, his uncle was a rather unpleasant man, and shortly after I was born he decided to switch to a career in sales. This was a better fit for his considerable interpersonal skills and offered him more autonomy to achieve his financial goals.

The post-war social and political climate for New York Jews leaned heavily Democratic and pro-labor with even some influence from the Communist Party USA. With his empathy for the 'working man', this was a good fit for him. He was a forceful debater and advocate for whatever he believed in and as best as I can determine was fairly active politically.

As he aged and started to accumulate some wealth his politics underwent a dramatic shift. While he still supported the economic agenda of the Democrats (Social Security and eventually Medicare) he became increasingly hostile to their social views. In particular, he felt that they 'kowtowed' to racial minorities. He was quite vociferous about this. He was also quite active. He organized groups to protest school busing and other liberal policies. He wasn't shy about speaking up in community and political settings and with his loud voice and strong opinions he was a force to be reckoned with.

When I was old enough to formulate my own views and able to articulate them they were uniformly in opposition to his. We would sometimes get into heated debates and even vitriolic shouting matches. I was convinced he was an unrepentant bigot and he saw me as naïve and overly idealistic. In his mind, I was someone whose views would ultimately be tempered by experience. These disagreements definitely put a strain on our relationship. But one night when I was 16 or 17, we had a very interesting interchange. We were sitting at the kitchen table for one of our dinner sessions. I started to tell him about a column I had just read that supported my point of view about some contentious issue we had been debating. Rather than take the bait and engage me on the topic he looked up and told me that he was really proud of me. He said that he typically felt that he prevailed in political debates but not with me. He said it made him happy and proud to see me get the better of him in argument. It was more important to him to have a son who could do this than to win the argument. Beyond the satisfaction of having my skills praised, at this moment I felt an incredibly strong bond with him.

In a similar vein, I remember once when Debbie was arguing with him about something she wanted. I joined in with her and the two of us relentlessly pressed the case. There was a moment when you could see his evident frustration give way to delight. He was happier that Debbie and I were allies than that he was now losing this fight.

When it was time to apply to colleges there were numerous opportunities for me. My academic record at the selective Stuyvesant High School was excellent. Although my father included some heavy-handed warnings about how I was expected to behave in college, he let me know that he would pay for college so I could focus on my studies. So many of my friends had to work part-time jobs. I was accepted everywhere I applied and decided to go to MIT, which was just about the most expensive school in the country. Just to keep this in perspective with the cost of college today, tuition was $1,900 when I arrived in the fall of 1966. It had just been raised from $1,750 sparking protests on campus with the chants of "1,900 too damn much." I wasn't sure though if his generosity and pride were about my accomplishments or because this school was the way to enhance my future earnings. Once in school, any discussion of which subject I would major in was always focused on its earning potential.

One moment of genuine pride however occurred about ten years later. After college, I had become enamored with the 'alternative school' movement. I got a Master's Degree in this field from Indiana University, which had a renowned program in this area. My father was none too thrilled by this turn of events. But after a few years of expanding the minds of my high school students in the areas of math and physics, I decided that the mind that needed expanding was my own. I went back to school to study engineering at the University Of Pennsylvania. By this time I had two young children, an old house in need of repair, and an increasingly unhappy wife. Despite all this, I earned a PhD in just three years. At my graduation, my father was beaming. No talk of money, just deep-seated, full-throated fatherly pride.

Dad and me at my PhD graduation

My dad had a keen interest in ham radio, which in the day was the only way to communicate over long distances. After he retired and moved to Florida he decided it was time to upgrade his equipment. He purchased a more powerful transceiver and installed a very tall antenna by the side of the house. What was interesting about this purchase, for which he seemed almost sheepish, was how unusual it was. For all that he focused on making and having money, he rarely spent any of it for himself. He had an extremely strong saving ethic. Virtually every dollar that was spent was for the benefit of one of the other family members or the family in general.

In response to the poverty of his childhood, he had an extreme aversion to acquiring anything that was used. Only brand new was good enough for him. While I know other people who, like my dad, would never buy a used car he is the only one who I have ever heard of who refused to consider a 'used house'. That's right, only new construction for him.

My dad had an unusual relationship with being Jewish. On one hand, he was not at all religious in any meaningful sense of the word. He was raised in a secular household, and had never studied the religion nor had a Bar Mitzvah. On the other hand, being Jewish completely defined him and his outlook on the world. Every news event was filtered through the lens of how it would impact the Jews. Even personal relationships were filtered through this lens.

I lived the classic secular Jewish lifestyle as I was growing up in my household. Absolutely no religious observance but full participation in the traditions. We gathered family and friends for Passover and the traditional 'break the fast' meal at the end of Yom Kippur, the holiest of holidays (even though we didn't fast). You could say that we were 'Gastro Jews'. I don't think my dad cared one way or the other, but my Mom insisted that I go to Hebrew school and become a Bar Mitzvah. For a while, I took my Jewish studies very seriously. Not just in the academic sense, but I tried on being a true believer. This didn't last too long and to this day I am a militant agnostic ("I don't know and neither do you!").

In my last year in college, I moved off campus into an apartment with three non-Jewish roommates. Other than nominating me to be the one who would deal with our Jewish landlady, this was of absolutely no consequence to any of us. However, my father kept checking with me that this arrangement was working out. He wanted to be sure that my roommates didn't mind living with a Jew and told me to alert him if (although I really think in his mind it was 'when') I ran into any trouble.

I had in fact run into anti-Semitic trouble earlier in my life. When I was 13 or 14 I had a newspaper delivery route. During the week the papers weren't too bulky and were easy to collect and deliver. The much larger

Sunday papers however presented more of a challenge. For the Sunday papers, I filled a two-wheel shopping cart that my mom normally used for grocery shopping. One day there was a delay in the printing of the newspapers so I had to go to the central distribution location to wait until they were ready. This site was in another neighborhood that was not heavily Jewish like mine. When I got there the other kids started taunting me. At first, it was only about my shopping cart. But it quickly escalated. They hurled vile anti-Semitic epithets my way and started pushing, shoving, and even spitting at me. When the newspapers finally arrived they proceeded to rip mine and scatter the sections around the street.

When I recovered and my tormenters had left, I called my dad. He came rushing over and was everything you would want your father to be. The perfect mix of advocate, empathizer (not something he normally practiced), and problem solver. He helped me reassemble the papers and then drove me to all my delivery stops. He even had examined my delivery list and made sure that the most damaged papers would go to our closest friends who would be the most forgiving. He then followed up with a call to not only the delivery manager but also the paper's managing editor. He emphatically let them know that things had to change. Through his forceful efforts, they changed the entire delivery protocol. From that point forward there was always a responsible adult present during the distribution process.

While I was away at college a large tract of land near our house was up for sale. An ultra-orthodox Hassidic Jewish community was one of the potential buyers. My dad was a leader of a group of neighbors that fought this sale. Through their efforts, the sale was in fact thwarted. I was stunned by the extraordinary hypocrisy in this. How could he rant and rave about how Jews were always being persecuted and had to stick together against the harsh anti-Semitic world out there and then turn around and do the exact same thing to these more religious Jews. His explanation of how different and insular they were sure didn't hold much water with me.

When Grandma Gussie died, my dad arranged for a 'rent-a-rabbi' to officiate at the service. While everyone was gathering in the chapel for the service I lingered behind and overheard him tell the rabbi, "Keep this brief. We don't believe in any of this."

Late in his life, my dad was in the hospital in Florida undergoing hip replacement surgery. Something went really wrong with the operation and he was in excruciating pain. He had to go back for a second surgery. I flew to Florida to be with him for this. When I got there he had just had the second surgery and seemed to be doing much better. More notable than his medical progress was how he was dealing with his hospital stay. He was a gregarious man who was always making friends and ingratiating himself with others. These were all skills that served him well as a salesman. When I went to check on him he made sure to introduce me to all of the nurses and support staff. He knew all their names and something about each of them. And they all seemed to love him too. He made sure my mom brought cake and drinks whenever she visited. It was almost like a party atmosphere. He gathered a bunch of the staff around his bed and said, "This is my son Joel. He is a wonderful father. I am not sure where he learned that since it wasn't from me." I was stunned. If he was referring to how much (or little) time he spent with his children, then this was clearly true. But with my dad, the love was always present. Even at the most trying times in our relationship, it was always there. I am not so sure he knew that though.

My dad lived large. Literally large. He was loud and gregarious and obese. I often wondered whether his overeating was compensation for a childhood of extreme poverty. But one thing is for sure, this wasn't healthy. He had trouble with his heart and developed diabetes in his 50's. By the time he was in his 60's, there was a succession of ailments that dominated his time and attention. He was battling congestive heart failure when he was hit with a cerebral stroke. He died at the age of 67. By that time I was completely independent of my parents and was a strong and capable man of 40 who had a family and a flourishing career. I was amazed at how lost and alone and unprotected I felt. My mom was still alive, but I felt like an orphan. It was an intense feeling that transcended grief.

As per his wishes, my dad was cremated and had his ashes spread over the Atlantic Ocean off the coast of Florida. Though of course I could and still did think about him quite a bit, I felt cheated out of a place to go visit him. I decided that the best way to connect with him was to visit the gravesites of his parents. My dad revered his parents. It seemed like the best way to stay in touch with him was through them.

In Florida at mom and dad's house circa 1983. Stuart and me standing, Mom with David and Dad with Jamie sitting

When Grandpa Jimmy died in 1952 the family was still quite poor. His grave plot was donated by the Pannonia Beneficial Society, a small Jewish charity. He is buried in an old and cramped Jewish cemetery in Fairview New Jersey in the section reserved for the beneficiaries of the charity. Not exactly a pauper's grave, but it spoke to the difficult circumstances in which he had lived.

Grandma Gussie lived much longer and didn't die until 1972. By then my dad was doing quite well financially and found a different Jewish cemetery in New Jersey for her. He loved the fact that this cemetery had numerous paths and trees and absolutely no headstones. Unless you looked down at the flush grave markers you would think you were in a peaceful country park. Using some kind of calculation about future usage that only made sense to him he purchased nine plots. As of today eight of them are still unused.

To get an idea of the impact my dad had on people, consider what happened the first time I visited Grandma Gussie's grave site. It was in 1990, 18 years after she had been buried. I dropped by the caretaker's house to ask where her grave was located. As soon as I mentioned her name he immediately asked if I was George's boy. 18 years after he had met him! To the best of my knowledge, they had just conducted the normal business of arranging the burial. This is a situation that the caretaker must have repeated hundreds if not thousands of times since. When I told him that George was indeed my dad, but that he had passed away the year before he seemed genuinely sad. This was just one, seemingly random person, who interacted with my dad. I was struck, and not for the first time, what an impression he made on people and what a memorable man he was.

Every year on the Sunday in April that is nearest to the anniversary of his death I drive up to northern New Jersey to visit these two cemeteries. It has become an important ritual in my life. When I get there I think of my grandparents. I think of my dad. I think of my dad's relationship with them. And I think of the two of us.

Chapter 4

The Search Begins

I pride myself on my ability to think clearly, analyze information and creatively explore possible solutions to whatever problems are in front of me. I had built a long and successful career creating data analysis software using just these skills. In this case, though, I wasn't sure where to begin.

I knew virtually nothing about DNA testing and hardly anything about the underlying theory of what exactly DNA is and how it is inherited. I couldn't tell you the difference between the terms DNA, chromosome, gene, or anything else related to the subject. Clearly, I had some serious learning in front of me.

This not only didn't faze me but I looked forward to tackling a new topic and mastering enough of the basics (and beyond if needed) to be able to use this technology to my advantage. I read several online articles about the subject and purchased a couple of books to help me along. Before long I could not only define and understand all of the terms I previously was clueless about but became quite adept at interpreting even the most technical aspects of a DNA test. Would you like to know what a 'Single Nucleotide Polymorphism' is?

So far so good. But......I still had no idea who my biological father was. Or for that matter how he got to be my father. What exactly happened in 1948 to conceive me? Did my mother have an affair? Was my conception the result of some form of artificial insemination? Did artificial insemination even exist in 1948? Regardless of what happened, did my father know what was going on? Or for that matter did something happen where even my mother wasn't sure what had transpired?

Neither of my parents was still alive when I made this discovery, so I couldn't ask them. There were also exceptionally few contemporaries of theirs still alive. And the very few who were still around were in their 90's and would most likely have hazy memories or for that matter any direct knowledge of what happened anyway. So the direct investigation of this was going to be difficult if not impossible.

There were however two additional avenues of inquiry that could be fruitful. The first, and most obvious one, was to scour my DNA results for as many 'close as possible' relatives to see if I could build a family tree that might somehow lead to the identity of my father. Once I was adept at interpreting the DNA results this was a very promising path to pursue.

My strategy was to look for people who were as closely related to me as possible but who were not related to Debbie. If I found a very close relative who was also related to Debbie then clearly that person was related to us on our mother's side. That might be nice to know but was not relevant to my current search.

I thought quite a bit about what a 'close enough relative' would be. Of course, I would be thrilled if I found another half-sibling. If I could communicate with my newfound sibling then I would immediately know who my father was. This was extremely unlikely. But maybe I could find a first cousin. That would be almost as good. After all, my father would be the brother of one of the parents of my first cousin. It would probably be fairly easy to figure it out from there.

But what about more distant relatives? How far removed from me would it even make sense to follow up on? Given my age, I was unlikely to find any aunts or uncles. If they were still alive they would be in their 90's and probably not actively pursuing their DNA results online. But what about more distant cousins?

I first had to solidify my understanding of exactly what these relationships were. A first cousin is someone who shares one of your two sets of grandparents with you. A second cousin is someone who shares one of your four sets of great grandparents with you. I could imagine that finding and talking to some of my paternal second cousins might be a good beginning on the path toward identifying who my biological father is.

29

Anything further removed than a second cousin however was very unlikely to be a fruitful avenue of inquiry. So my strategy was to find and contact as many paternal second cousins as I could and see what I could make out of all that. By the way, the term 'cousin once removed' just means that he or she is a generation older or younger than the cousin in question. For example, a second cousin once removed would be the parent or child of your second cousin. They would also be of interest to me.

Despite the clarity I had about pursuing this strategy there were a few hurdles to overcome. The first and most daunting was the likelihood that whoever I found just wouldn't have any relevant information for me. Or more fundamentally might not even be interested or available to respond to my inquiries.

The second was the imprecision in the DNA results. The further removed from you a relative is the less precise the results are. You could be fairly certain about how to interpret the results of parents, children, siblings, half-siblings, and maybe even first cousins. After that, it is quite a bit fuzzier. So that means you might be pursuing someone who based on the DNA results you believe to be your second cousin, but in reality, is a more distant relative who just so happens to share more DNA than would typically be the case. I learned very quickly to take every finding as provisional until it could be independently verified.

The final hurdle was the easiest to remedy. By just looking through the results on 23andMe I was limiting myself only to people who had also purchased and sent in a 23andMe DNA kit. As it turns out there are several other popular DNA testing companies. By submitting a testing kit to each of them I would be expanding the potential pool of relatives I might find. The other major companies I decided to join are Ancestry, Family Tree, and My Heritage. They each have their advantages and disadvantages. But collectively they offered a much larger universe of possible matches. For my current purposes, the one I was the most interested in was Ancestry, because it had by far the largest database of users. It was mid-June by the time I realized all this and was ready to register with these sites. Ironically they were all running half-price 'Father's Day' sales then.

The approach I was taking was one I was well prepared for. In my career, I developed data analysis software and became quite adept at examining data and letting it guide me to what the conclusion ought to be. I was comfortable with this approach and didn't even imagine that there might be another way to go.

However, I was soon presented with an alternative strategy. My daughter-in-law Erin forwarded me a link to an episode of the radio program and podcast 'This American Life'. She told me that my story was remarkably similar to one she had heard there. I immediately listened to the episode and my jaw just about hit the floor.

The podcast was the story of Lennard Davis, a man who, just like me, was raised by a lower-middle-class Jewish couple in the Bronx. He was 6 months younger than me and found out late in life that the father who raised him was not his biological father. The story he told included many interesting details about his family dynamics and also how he used DNA evidence to search for his biological father. I was fascinated. At the end of the podcast, they made mention of the fact that he had written the book, 'Go Ask Your Father', about his experience. In two minutes I had his book on my Kindle and was avidly reading about this remarkable coincidence.

In the book he goes on at some length about the practices of 'fertility specialists' circa 1948. It was amazing to see what they both knew and didn't know about fertility matters back then. The doctors claimed that there was a much greater likelihood of a woman successfully getting pregnant if the man's sperm were inserted into her with a syringe rather than from the man's penis. They even had a marketing slogan: "A 3-inch head start for a 6-inch journey." While the efficacy of this approach is debatable, there was no question that these doctors did somehow show improved odds for conceiving a baby.

According to Lennard Davis, this was much more likely because a donor's sperm might be involved. He spent a fair amount of time and energy, not to mention thought trying to see if his mother's gynecologist was really his biological father. His speculation was fueled by the fact that his mom saw a highly regarded gynecologist in Manhattan rather than a local doctor in the Bronx. Though I had never thought it noteworthy, I had always known that that was also the case for my mom. He ultimately discovered that the doctor was not his father.

But it did make me think about my situation. Might I be the product of donor insemination from someone hired by the doctor or by the doctor himself? This was an extremely intriguing idea to contemplate.

There were several different scenarios in which it might have happened. The one that captured my imagination involved mixing the sperm from a donor with that of my dad's. This would increase the odds of conception while also muddying the waters regarding exactly who the actual father was. In 1948 there was no ability to freeze sperm. So this rather unorthodox mixing would have to happen in real-time. Both the husband and the donor would have to be present at the same time for this to work. That doesn't mean however that they would actually meet each other or for that matter that the husband would even know what was going on.

I have a vivid imagination. I couldn't help but picturing this playing out as it would in a classic British mistaken identity comedy. These are the ones where everyone is confused as people keep shifting locations with doors opening and shutting all over the place. All of this was being done in the service of keeping an important secret.

To further complicate the issue the doctors believed (altogether logically) that repeating the process a second and even a third time in consecutive days would greatly improve the chances of success. This meant that the elaborate merging of the sperm from a donor (there was no guarantee that it would be the same man each time) and the husband had to be repeated. This was problematic because it involved making sure that a donor was ready, willing, and able to perform his part of the job at just the right time on consecutive days.

Naturally, this didn't always work out. If a timely donor wasn't available the doctor had some difficult choices to make. He could use some pretext to cancel the session. Obviously, this wouldn't sit well with the couple who had arranged their schedules to be there. He could proceed with just the husband's sperm. This would seem to the couple like a normal session. Of course, it lacked the extra 'juice' that the sperm mixing provided.

And there was another option. The doctor could become the donor. He could mix his own sperm with the husband's and proceed from there. It is not at all clear how often this happened. And it is not clear how many doctors actually started with this option rather than even try to find another donor. What is clear is that sometimes it did happen.

There were also other possibilities that didn't involve any nefarious sperm mixing going on. Perhaps the doctor was completely above board and offered my parents his services as a donor. Perhaps he told my mom what he was doing but my dad was in the dark. Perhaps he tricked my mom by inserting his sperm into her with a syringe as part of a 'treatment'. Perhaps he had an affair with my mom. Perhaps....perhaps....perhaps. My mind was reeling with the possibilities.

I knew this was a long shot not based on any existing evidence but I nonetheless decided to make this my second avenue of attack. Instead of gathering the data that the DNA testing provided and seeing where it led, I would play a hunch and invert the process. I would start with a tentative conclusion (my mom's gynecologist was my father) and then look for information to support it.

So off I went working on both methodologies at the same time. Whenever there was a lull in one approach I increased my attention on the other. In my view, the data-driven approach was the 'right' way to do this. Examine the data as they are uncovered, double-check your results, and move ahead as the information warranted. The other approach seemed like a quixotic attempt to add some fun and excitement to what could easily become a slow and tedious task. The mixture of the two was a way to keep the overall momentum going when one or the other of the approaches hit a snag.

Chapter 5

That's Not All

As momentous an event in my life as this DNA mystery was it might not even have been the biggest thing going on for me at the time. Ten months before my shocking DNA discovery I had been diagnosed with Multiple Myeloma. Myeloma is the second most common type of blood cancer (after Non-Hodgkin's Lymphoma). Despite that, it is a very rare form of cancer. According to the American Cancer Society, in the US there are about 32,000 new cases of myeloma a year. The lifetime risk of getting myeloma is only about 0.75%. It is a very complex disease to understand and treat and for which there is no cure.

In July of 2017, I was feeling just fine and had my annual physical. A few days later my doctor called and told me that my blood work looked odd. I had a condition called pancytopenia, which means that all my blood counts were low. She recommended that I see a hematologist to get it checked out. When I asked for a recommendation, she told me that she had already made an appointment for me. This sounded serious.

After consultation with the hematologist, lots more blood tests, and a bone marrow biopsy I was conclusively diagnosed with Multiple Myeloma. When I heard this I had absolutely no idea what this disease was. I think I might have ever heard the word 'myeloma', but even that I wasn't sure about. Maybe it was 'melanoma' that I had run across. What was this disease? What was my life going to be like living with it? And how long could I expect to live with it?

My entire being was transformed after the diagnosis. Everything I was doing or planning to do was pushed aside so that I could understand and deal with my cancer. This was my focus. I really couldn't process the implication of this without understanding all there was to know about the disease. For me information is power. So I set out to gain that power.

I learned that myeloma is a cancer of the plasma cells in the bone marrow. When healthy, these cells produce antibodies called immunoglobulins that fight different types of infections. Myeloma cells over reproduce an abnormal antibody that is not only useless in fighting infections but also tends to crowd out all the other types of blood cells. That is what had caused my pancytopenia. Besides reducing the body's immune function, the myeloma cells disrupt the normal bone-building and bone-breakdown cycle, causing more destruction and less building. In many people, myeloma is discovered only after it has first caused some serious bone problems. Another potential problem area is in the kidneys. Excessive calcium generated from the disrupted bone cycle or even fragments of the myeloma antibodies called light chains can cause serious kidney dysfunction.

When I received the diagnosis from the hematologist on the phone, her first words were "You're lucky it is 2017." In the previous ten years, there had been huge advances in the so-called 'novel' treatments for the disease. A surprisingly large number of new medications for such a rare disease had been tested and approved and were showing promising signs of prolonging life. Regardless of this good news, I was really taken aback by the very first thing I read about the disease. According to the American Cancer Society, the median life expectancy for someone with myeloma was 61 months. I literally shook when I read this.

Unlike my experience learning about DNA to better understand my lineage, I had a really hard time mastering this subject. It was undeniably complex. It was filled with abstruse medical terminology and a seemingly infinite supply of acronyms. But it was me more than the subject matter. I found it difficult to focus and absorb and remember whatever I was reading, seeing, or hearing. I was adrift. I read and re-read the same articles while only gaining a little bit more understanding each time. I grew frustrated with the snail's pace of my knowledge gain.

I had been in one of my off periods in therapy when I received the diagnosis but immediately started up again to figure out how to deal with this. In addition to my individual therapy, I found and contacted a

Philadelphia-based myeloma support group. Before I got to go to any meetings I spoke with one of the group's founders. He described all that he had been through in terms of the disease and its treatments for the past 20 years. Listening to his calm assurances and upbeat attitude put this disease into a better perspective. It felt like I could now exhale and clear my mind so I could begin to understand what I needed. With the fog lifted I dove into the deep end and read voraciously, attended seminars in person and online, and asked my doctor many, many questions. Unlike tech support at 23andMe, he seemed to enjoy my numerous and increasingly detailed questions.

One of the things that I learned very early on is the value of being treated by a myeloma specialist. It is a complex disease with a very rapidly changing treatment landscape. There was one study that showed that patients who saw a specialist (even as a consult) lived on average almost 40% longer than those who were treated only by a hematologist or general oncologist. There are probably only a few hundred of these specialists in the entire country. I was very fortunate that there were several to choose from at the Abramson Cancer Center at Penn here in Philadelphia.

The good news for me when I started treatment is that there was no evidence of any bone or kidney damage at all. Our job was to halt and then reduce the level of the disease before any damage could occur. I was immediately put on the recommended course of treatment. This included two medications by pill and a weekly injection. The statistics looked promising. This treatment regimen was effective for close to 90% of patients. But as they say in those fast-talking automotive ads, "your mileage may vary."

Taking these medications made me worse off than when I started. My myeloma numbers were slightly (but just slightly) better but the side effects of the medications were brutal. I was constantly fatigued in a way I had never felt before. This was different than just being tired. It was all-consuming. One day a week I took a high dose of steroids that was supposed to enhance the other medications. For the next two days instead of fatigue, I was completely wired. Absolutely no sleep led to even more fatigue when its effects wore off. And for good measure I was neutropenic. This meant that I had very low white blood counts and was susceptible to infection. For fucks sake, this was the very condition we were trying to overcome! After three months, I had gone from sick but feeling fine to being just as sick but feeling terrible.

We switched to a second course of treatment that involved a weekly hour-long infusion of one of the medications. This went somewhat better than the first round. The side effects weren't quite as bad and it actually made a small but noticeable reduction in my myeloma. However, it stopped being effective after three more months.

So after six months I had had a modest and no longer improving reduction in my disease and was feeling fatigued and discouraged. So we switched yet again and began a third treatment regimen. This included a relatively new medication that had to be administered in a five-hour infusion. At first weekly, and then bi-weekly, and after 24 weeks total it would only be monthly. Amazingly this worked. My myeloma numbers started to drop and the side effects were much less pronounced. And at just this time I joined the LiveStrong program at my local Y. This is a physical fitness program for cancer patients and survivors that includes individualized workout routines and group sessions to share our experiences. The combination of progress in my treatment and feeling much healthier and vital due to the gym workouts dramatically lifted my spirits.

At this point, I had an important decision to make. The standard of care for myeloma patients, after successful induction treatment that reduces the disease to a manageable level, is to undergo a procedure called a stem cell transplant. In this procedure, you are administered a massive amount of a chemotherapy drug that completely kills all of the cells in your bone marrow. Then a new batch of stem cells is added into your bloodstream to begin the process of repopulating the marrow.

There are two main types of stem cell transplants: autologous and allogeneic. In an autologous transplant, the stem cells are collected from your own blood prior to the procedure. In an allogeneic transplant, the stem cells come from a donor. Since there is a substantial risk of rejecting a donor's stem cells, the allogeneic transplant is only performed in exceptional situations. In the autologous transplant, there is a risk that you will be reintroducing some of the cancer cells that you already have along with the stem cells. For a while, it was considered best practice to try and purge these cancer cells before the stem cells were returned to your body. Interestingly, studies have shown that there really weren't any additional benefits from doing this. So they are typically added back as is.

Keeping in mind that there is no cure, studies do show that an autologous stem cell transplant is the most likely way to provide the deepest and longest-lasting response. However, it also involves a lengthy and onerous hospital stay with a recovery that typically lasts several months. There is considerable debate in the myeloma community as to whether or not this is still necessary. The plethora of novel agents is proving to be quite effective at reducing the disease without a transplant. However, they are so new that it hasn't been possible yet to assess their long-term efficacy versus a transplant.

Even if you decide not to undergo a transplant, it is recommended that you 'harvest' and then freeze your stem cells just in case you opt for one at a later date. Stem cells are normally found in the bone marrow. To harvest them they have to be coaxed out of the marrow and into the blood. From there, an apheresis machine can extract them from the body. This process is very similar to that used for kidney dialysis. In this case, the blood is circulated from your body through the machine that extracts the stem cells and then back in again. A typical session lasts a few hours. Often one sitting is enough, Many people harvest enough stem cells in one sitting, but it took me three days to get enough.

Several days before the apheresis you have to inject yourself with medications that excite the stem cells and get them to leave the bone marrow and circulate in the blood. Both the professional literature and the anecdotal evidence provided by my friends who had gone through with harvesting indicated that this part of the process was not particularly onerous. I was fine with the self-injections and the apheresis itself, but I was not fine with the aftermath. Almost immediately I felt fatigued with a low level but constant queasiness. It just never went away. Unfortunately, it was worst when I was lying down. Nausea medications didn't help. This lasted many, many weeks and completely undid the buoyant feeling I had from my newfound physical fitness routine.

It turns out there is one way to be distracted from incessant queasiness. Just two weeks after the apheresis, Debbie's DNA results were posted and my identity, queasy or otherwise, was upended.

And at the same time, our 17-year-old Spanish Water Dog Lucia was so unable to live any semblance of a normal dog's life that we had to have her euthanized. So sad and for me a reminder of the mortality that faces us all.

I ultimately decided to undergo a stem cell transplant. The data about its benefits, while not overwhelming, were persuasive enough to convince me that I would get the best chance at a longer-lasting remission. I was hoping that the procedure would yield a complete response and afford me several years before the almost inevitable relapse.

Susan and I had late spring and early summer plans already in place so I scheduled the transplant for the very end of July. The first day in the hospital I was administered a very large dose of an old-line chemotherapy drug that completely wipes out everything in the bone marrow. Not only the myeloma cells but also all the good plasma cells and even the stem cells that can repopulate the marrow. On day three, my harvested stem cells were thawed and reinserted into my body so that I could have a fresh start. It takes a few days for them to find their way into the bone marrow and then several more for them to implant, reproduce and start to generate new healthy blood cells. During this period you basically have no immune system, no energy, and no appetite. Only the daily cajoling and threats from the dietician could make me eat even a minimal amount. I was in the hospital for 17 days and left it weakened, diarrheic, considerably lighter, and bald.

Back home after the transplant without any hair but with my two sons David and Jamie

At three months I got the official test results that showed there were no traces of any myeloma markers in my blood. It was a complete response to the treatment and I was officially in remission. At this point, I could just sit back and enjoy life or undergo maintenance treatment to try and prolong the remission as long as possible. I elected to resume the treatments that had been so effective and which had had relatively minor side effects. Of course, I don't know how this will turn out. As I finalize this book it has been three years since my transplant and I am feeling cautiously upbeat about the future. So much so that we went out and got a new puppy! Sofia is now along for the ride.

Chapter 6

How Do You Even Spell DNA?

When I first received my 23andMe DNA results I was eager to see if there might be some close and interesting relatives with whom I could connect. Even before Debbie's results came back one name stood out among all the others. At the top of my list was someone named David Levine. According to the 23andMe analysis, he was my closest relative and most likely my second cousin. I was intrigued but didn't initially do anything to contact him and explore exactly how we were related.

After Debbie's results were posted and especially after we received cousin Roy's results, there was a new urgency about contacting possible 'close enough' relatives.

The report showed that David Levine and I shared 4.26% of our DNA across 12 different segments. Clearly, 23andMe thought that was significant enough for us to be considered second cousins. But was that the only possibility? Could 4.26% be enough to indicate that we might be even more closely related than second cousins? Or could it be a fluke and we were really more distant relatives? And what in the world was the significance of 12 segments? Is that a lot or a little? What exactly is a segment and how many of them could there be?

To add to the situation, Debbie also sent a DNA sample to Ancestry. There were two reasons for this. First, to completely and absolutely be sure that the 23andMe results were reproduced by another company whose analysis was completely independent. Second, it would allow me to use the very large Ancestry database to search for DNA relatives who I knew for sure were unrelated to Debbie.

It wasn't surprising (though deep, deep inside of me disappointing) that the Ancestry results matched the 23andMe results. Half siblings, we were. Interestingly my top relative on Ancestry (not counting Debbie) was none other than David Levine. It seems he really gets around. The Ancestry report was structured differently than the 23andMe report. While it also predicted the most likely relationship, it didn't offer a percentage of matching DNA. Instead, it showed the amount of shared DNA along with the number of segments. In this report, David Levine and I shared 295 centimorgans (cm) of DNA across 15 segments and we were predicted to be 2nd to 3rd cousins.

While it was pretty straightforward to understand what the sharing percentage in the 23andMe report meant, I had no clue what a 'centimorgan' was. My first guess is that there must have been a genetics pioneer named Morgan and that a centimorgan was 1/100 of a full Morgan. It turns out that this glib analysis was half right. Thomas Hunt Morgan was indeed a genetics pioneer for whom the unit is named. However, the 'centi' part of the name was something else altogether. The entry for centimorgan in Wikipedia explains that it is defined as "the distance between chromosome positions for which the expected average number of intervening chromosomal crossovers in a single generation is 0.01." Huh? Clearly, this was going to get really complex really quickly.

Even for me, I had to decide where to draw the line between developing a deep understanding and learning just enough for the information to be useful. Though I found the topic extremely interesting and had an inclination to pursue it to become a lay expert, this seemed like it would take quite a bit of time and effort. I decided instead to see if I could find the sweet spot where I knew enough to be comfortable with all the terminology without having to invest a huge amount of time mastering it all.

After some fits and starts, I reached a point where I felt like I achieved this goal. My key takeaways were:

- A person's DNA is contained inside the nucleus of virtually every cell in the human body.

- This DNA consists of approximately 3 billion 'base pairs' of connected nucleic acids (called nucleotides) split across 23 chromosomes.
- Approximately 99.9% of the nucleotides are the same in every person.
- The ones that can vary are what determine a person's characteristics. These are called SNP's (Single Nucleotide Polymorphisms).
- A matching segment of DNA for two people is a consecutive set of nucleotides that are the same.
- Since any two people will match on 99.9% of the base pairs in a segment, the only thing of interest is how many SNP's there are in the matching segment. This quantity is measured in centimorgans (cm).
- A person's complete set of genes is called a genome.
- There are approximately 6,800 centimorgans in a person's genome.

23andMe only considers segments of 7 cm or greater to be matching, while the cutoff for Ancestry is 5 cm. That is why Ancestry reported that David Levine and I shared 15 segments while 23andMe had only 12.

Even though Ancestry didn't report a shared DNA percentage, it is easily calculated. The 295 cm of shared DNA is 4.34% of the total amount of 6,800.

With all this knowledge in hand, I awaited the results from the other two DNA companies. When I got my results back from FamilyTree they were yet again different in format. Like Ancestry they showed the total number of shared centimorgans instead of a percentage. But instead of counting up the number of shared segments they only listed the length in centimorgans of the longest segment. Why did they do this? Was this a significant indicator of how closely related two people would be? Why did they omit the number of segments and for that matter why did the other companies not mention the largest segment? The questions never seemed to end.

My final set of results were from MyHeritage. These hit the jackpot of information. They showed percentages, shared centimorgans, the number of segments, and the largest segment.

The first step in understanding the significance of the amount of DNA I shared with someone was to know what the expected value was for each possible relationship. I already knew that siblings would expect to share 50% of their DNA and that half-siblings only 25%. But what about first cousins, second cousins, etc.? The International Society of Genetic Genealogy has created a very useful chart with these values.

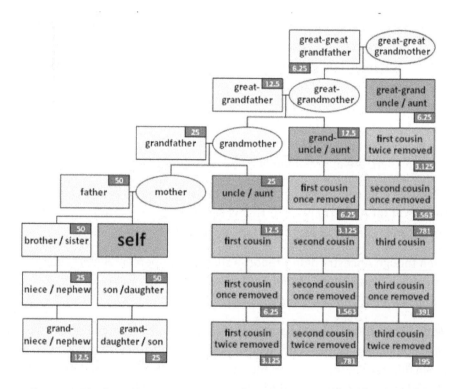

The expected value of shared DNA. Source: International Society of Genetic Genealogy

As we can see in this chart, the expected value for shared DNA for second cousins is 3.125%. So, if David Levine and I really shared approximately 4.3% of our DNA then it would seem very likely that we were indeed second cousins. But is this the only possibility? The problem with the expected values in the chart is just that, they are 'expected'. What I really wanted to see were actual ranges of what was likely for each relationship. As it turns out this information already exists.

The Shared CM Project set about collecting real-world information about shared DNA from people with known relationships. They wound up collecting information from over 25,000 people. Using this information, they created a similar chart to the theoretical one. For each relationship, their chart shows the actual average amount in cm of the shared DNA as well as the range of values that were found.

The Shared cM Project – Version 3.0 (August 2017)

Figure 1. The Relationship Chart

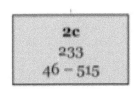

The Shared cM Project – Version 3.0 August 2017

Blaine T. Bettinger
www.TheGeneticGenealogist.com
CC 4.0 Attribution License

For MUCH more information (including histograms and company breakdowns) see: goo.gl/Z1EcJQ

How to read this chart:

Aunt/Uncle	← Relationship
1750	← Average
1349 - 2175	← Range (low-high) (99% Percentile)

Half GG-Aunt/Uncle 187 13 - 383				Great-Grandparent 881 464 - 1486					Great-Great Aunt/Uncle 427 191 - 885		Other Relationships
	Half Great-Aunt/Uncle 432 125 - 765			Grandparent 1766 1156 - 2311				Great Aunt/Uncle 914 251 - 2108			6C 21 0 - 86
		Half Aunt/Uncle 891 500 - 1446		Parent 3487 3330 - 3720		Aunt/Uncle 1750 1349 - 2175					6C1R 16 0 - 72
Half 3c 61 0 - 178	Half 2c 117 9 - 397	Half 1C 457 137 - 856	Half-Sibling 1783 1317 - 2312	Sibling 2629 2209 - 3384	SELF	1C 874 553 - 1225	2c 233 46 - 515	3c 74 0 - 217	4c 35 0 - 127	5c 25 0 - 94	6C2R 17 0 - 75
Half 3c1R 42 0 - 165	Half 2c1R 73 0 - 341	Half 1C1R 226 57 - 530	Half Niece/Nephew 891 500 - 1446	Niece/Nephew 1750 1349 - 2175	Child 3487 3330 - 3720	1C1R 439 141 - 851	2c1R 123 0 - 316	3C1R 48 0 - 173	4C1R 28 0 - 117	5C1R 21 0 - 79	7C 13 0 - 57
Half 3c2R 34 0 - 96	Half 2c2R 61 0 - 353	Half 1C2R 145 27 - 360	Half Great Niece/Nephew 432 125 - 765	Great-Niece/Nephew 910 251 - 2108	Grandchild 1766 1156 - 2311	1C2R 229 43 - 531	2c2R 74 0 - 261	3C2R 35 0 - 116	4C2R 22 0 - 109	5C2R 17 0 - 43	7C1R 13 0 - 53
Half 3c3R	Half 2c3R	Half 1C3R 87 0 - 191	Half GG Niece/Nephew 187 12 - 383	Great-Great-Niece/Nephew 427 191 - 885	Great-Grandchild 881 464 - 1486	1C3R 123 0 - 283	2c3R 57 0 - 139	3C3R 22 0 - 69	4C3R 29 0 - 82	5C3R 11 0 - 44	8C 12 0 - 50

Minimum was automatically set to 0 cM for relationships more distant than Half 2C, and averages were determined only for submissions in which DNA was shared

For example, in this chart, the actual average for 2nd cousins is 233 cm with a range of values from 46 to 515.

2c
233
46 – 515

45

Using this chart I could get a better sense of what possible relationships there might be for each potential relative. For example, David Levine and I shared 295 cm of our DNA. While that fits very nicely near the average for 2nd cousins it was also possible that he could be my 1st cousin once removed.

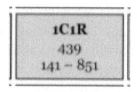

This could prove useful when (or if!) I was able to make contact with any of my relatives. It could help me figure out the correct relationship and help me point the way to finding my biological father.

Admittedly I could have ignored all these details and simply used the estimated relationship status that each test offered. After all, that was the service they were providing. As you can tell by now, that is not who I am. I really need to dig deep and have a grounds up understanding of the underlying concepts for anything important in my life. That is the only way that I feel in control of the situation. And just as importantly I derive quite a bit of satisfaction in learning something new.

Chapter 7

First Contact

Now that I felt empowered and ready to go, the first step was to find out if David Levine was related to me on my father's side or my mother's side. Before doing this I realized that from the first moment I saw his name I had always just assumed (for no good reason) that he was on my father's side.

There is a feature in the 23andMe website where you can get a list of common relatives. So I used that to see what common relatives David and I might have. My heart sank when I saw that Debbie was on this list. This indicated that she was related to both of us, and thus David would be related to me on my mother's side. Upon closer examination, however, it was clear that she wasn't really related to David. The listing showed that Debbie and David shared 0.15% of their DNA and were categorized as distant cousins. This was such a small number that there was no chance that they were related in any meaningful sense. The reality is, if you go back far enough, you could match virtually any Eastern European Jew with any other one as a distant cousin. This is undoubtedly what was happening here. I breathed a sigh of relief now knowing that David had to be related to me on my father's side.

With this information in hand, I decided to reach out to David to better understand exactly who he was and how we were related. There is an internal messaging system on the 23andMe site that I could use to contact him. I wrestled with what I should say to him. If I just went with a brief "hello, let's chat" message I thought it might not catch his interest. On the other hand, if I told him everything that was going on it might overwhelm him. I mulled this over and sought Susan's opinion. She was of the mind that the story is so interesting that including it would be more likely to elicit a response. I agreed and on May 28th, just 3 days after Debbie and I made our momentous discovery I sent the following message to him:

Hi David

I recently joined 23andMe and noticed that there is a very strong likelihood that we are 2nd cousins sharing a set of great grandparents. I am writing to see if you would be interested in exploring this possible connection with me.

My interest in making this connection goes beyond just the typical curiosity in finding previously unknown relatives. In a real shock to me, I have just found out that my sister is most likely just my half-sister. That means we share a mother but are from different fathers. This is completely contrary to what I have known and how I have lived my life. If all this is true, it means I do not know who my biological father is.

To make this more interesting, the DNA results from the site indicate that not only are you and I 2nd cousins but that we are related on my father's side. So you represent the first chance I would have to find out not only close or distant relatives but also perhaps the identity of my biological father.

I know this sounds a bit amazing.....but it is even more amazing to me. I am hoping you can help. Even if you don't have much information immediately available I would love to hear back from you and start exploring this together.

Thank you so much for considering all this.

Joel Gottfried

I anxiously awaited his reply. For some reason, I thought he would be obsessively refreshing his 23andMe page as often as I was. The reality of course could be that he had only a casual interest in the site. Or he might have joined it years ago and was no longer an active member. On June 13, after two excruciating weeks without a reply, I tried again. This time I thought the minimalist approach might be better:

Hi David

Following up on a previous message I sent. I would love to make contact with you. I have some very puzzling DNA results and am hoping you can help me figure them out.

Thanks so much for connecting with me. – Joel Gottfried

48

Again I waited for a reply, but none was forthcoming. On June 27 however, my Ancestry results arrived and David was listed as my closest relative on there as well. I figured I would give it a try to contact him there. Perhaps he was more active or attentive to messages on this site. Also, Ancestry had many more features to help you connect with potential relatives than just DNA results. Unlike 23andMe which was just focused on DNA testing, Ancestry was a full-service genealogical site used by many people who never even get their DNA tested. They have historical records, search tools, and family tree authoring and sharing capabilities. Based on the discretion of its author a family tree can be public and searchable or kept as private and only selectively shared.

David's entry in Ancestry indicated that he was part of a very large, but private family tree. This seemed like it could be a gold mine for me. On June 30 I sent him a very brief request to connect. A few days later he actually replied. I finally had my first contact with a possible new relative! Unfortunately, his message just pointed me to the family tree that I was unable to access because of its privacy settings. So tantalizingly close to getting some real information, yet so far.

If I was a 'glass half full' type of guy I would be celebrating that I now had made my first contact. If I was a 'glass half empty' type of guy I would be despairing that I knew absolutely nothing more than when I started. I was just glad that I was doing something even if it hadn't yet yielded any tangible results. Not to get too Meta about it, but I was glad I even had a glass that could contain the other metaphors that I could fill in whatever way I chose.

Chapter 8

What About The Doctor?

Since I was having such little luck making contact with my DNA relatives (actually just David Levine) I figured I might as well get to work on my other proposed line of inquiry. Who was my mother's gynecologist and might he have been involved in my conception (in more than the conventional way!)? I retrieved my birth certificate from my files and saw that I was delivered at Doctors Hospital by Dr. Nathan Mintz, whose listed address was 955 Park Avenue in Manhattan.

Doctors Hospital was founded in 1930 as a for-profit hospital that according to contemporaneous reports was considered to be a "fashionable treatment center for the well-to-do." It was on East End Avenue right across from Gracie Mansion, the mayor's official residence. It was nicknamed the 'hotel hospital' for its lavish interiors and family-style suites. Even when it transferred its assets to a public charity and became a non-profit hospital in 1940 the city of New York insisted it still owed property taxes because it only catered to well-off patients and didn't accept any charity cases. The hospital finally won this battle in the State Supreme Court but never changed its approach to medical care. Some of its more prominent patients (excluding my mother and me of course!) included Michael Jackson, Marilyn Monroe, Jacqueline Susann, James Thurber, Clare Boothe Luce, Eugene O'Neill, and Robert Mueller (yes that Robert Mueller....perhaps we can thank the doctors at this hospital for his vitality and good health today).

The hospital was acquired by the Beth Israel Medical Center in 1987 and eventually was closed in 2004. The building was razed the next year and luxury residences now occupy its prime real estate.

Doctors Hospital Inc.
170 East End Avenue
New York 28, N. Y.

March 29, 1949

Mrs. Tina Gottfried
Room 1040

March 20, 1949 to March 29, 1949 (11 AM)

Room 9 days at $9.00	$81.00
Floor Nurses	27.00
Nursery	16.00
Delivery Room & Obs. Anaes.	25.00
Pharmacy	5.02
	154.02
Less Deposit	100.00
	54.02
Less Hospital Insurance	80.00
(10 days at $8.00)	
Refund	$25.98

DOCTORS HOSPITAL
MAR 29 1949
PAID

JOEL

The "hotel hospital" wasn't so expensive after all!

The first question that popped into my mind was "What was a lower-middle-class woman from the Bronx doing at this hospital for the stars?" The most obvious answer was that this is where her doctor, Nathan Mintz, had admitting privileges. But that just pushes the question down the road a bit. "What was a lower-middle-class woman from the Bronx doing as a patient of a prominent Park Avenue Obstetrician/Gynecologist?"

He certainly wasn't the closest doctor to her. It would have taken her almost an hour each way by public transportation just for an office visit. This is someone she quite intentionally sought out and felt was worth seeing despite the time, effort, and expense.

51

So who was Nathan Mintz?

Through the magic of Google and the historical records in the Ancestry database, it was fairly easy to assemble the outlines of his life story. He was born in New York in 1912 to Louis and Bessie Mintz. He was the middle child, with an older brother Murray and a younger sister Gertrude.

Nathan attended NYU as an undergraduate and then immediately after graduation began at its medical school. In those days it was called the University and Bellevue Hospital Medical College. As best I can tell he graduated from NYU as an undergraduate in 1931 at the age of 19 and then from medical school in 1934 at the age of 22. This is remarkably young to have become a doctor. It is possible that NYU had a combined BS/MD program to allow such quick matriculation, but nonetheless, this is quite an impressive feat.

After graduating from medical school in 1934 he joined the OB/GYN department at Mt. Sinai Hospital and worked there for 60 years. This is also an impressive number. That is a really, really long time to be affiliated with anything……be it a job, friends, a house, or even a spouse!

If he was on staff at Mt. Sinai why then was I delivered at Doctors Hospital? Regardless of how I was conceived, there shouldn't have been anything unusual about the delivery. I do know that my mother thought this was a very special hospital. Maybe the difference in cost between it and Mt. Sinai wasn't so great that after 6 long years of not conceiving she and my dad felt they could splurge. In my imagination, however, there was Nathan Mintz, my biological father insisting that only the best would do for his son!

My mother was so enamored of the hospital that Debbie was born there three years later and my little brother Stuart ten years later. And as it turns out they were also delivered by Nathan Mintz. In fact, in 1964 when we were living in Queens, my mom needed a D&C and insisted that it be done only at Doctors Hospital. I remember her making a point about this. At the time of her visit to the hospital, I was attending Stuyvesant High School, which was also in Manhattan. The day after the surgery I took the bus uptown after school to visit her while she was recovering. I was struck by how expansive she was about the wonders of the place. I knew nothing about the hospital, but she made it a point to tell me about the luxury of the room and the great facilities. This loquaciousness was very atypical for her. She was usually a "just the facts ma'am" type of woman. There really was a story to this hospital. I just didn't know what it was.

She even raved about the food and insisted that I stay for dinner. To my unsophisticated teenage palate, it did seem to be an excellent meal. I was there for several hours and interacted with several hospital staff members during this time. Because the procedure was performed at Doctor's hospital, I assume that Nathan Mintz was the doctor performing it. Although I have absolutely no memory that it occurred, it is entirely possible that I met him while I was there.

What I really wanted was a copy of the medical records that Dr. Mintz kept of his time treating my mom. I figured that this was a long shot at best but I set out to see if they still existed. Though I found out that there were no longer any copies of his patient records, I got quite excited when I discovered that there was a biography of him buried somewhere in the Mt. Sinai archives. On June 27 I contacted the archivist and she retrieved it for me. For the couple of days I was waiting for this to arrive, my mind raced with possibilities. I was sure it would detail the doctor's groundbreaking infertility work and perhaps even lead to another stash of more detailed records. You can imagine my disappointment when the supposed 'biography' was nothing more than a couple of boilerplate paragraphs that the hospital president delivered in a ceremony in 1984 honoring Dr. Mintz on the occasion of his 50th anniversary at the hospital. Oh well.

As I continued my search, I did find a very revealing piece of information about the good doctor. In 1946 he attended a conference in Princeton, New Jersey called the 'Problem Of Fertility'. The papers presented at this conference were all about better understanding animal fertility, and infertility. These were presented as a way to gain insight into the same issues in humans. In 1946 there might not have been an official specialty focusing on infertility treatments, but Dr. Nathan Mintz did seem to have a professional interest in it.

I was also able to locate the yearbook from his final year in medical school. Next to each graduate's picture was a pithy description of the student. For Nathan it read:

Euphoric, euphonic and polysyllabic. Never minces his words. Is a big muscle man from the Bronx. Never fails to muscle in ahead of you in any clinic. Is the only one in the section who ever saw a skin lesion.

I was starting to like this guy!

I closely examined his yearbook picture to see if there might be a resemblance with me. I studied it and studied it but couldn't make up my mind. As a side note, however, I am famously bad at this. Everyone I know, and I mean everyone, says that my son Jamie and I look amazingly alike. So much so that when a life-sized blowup of a picture of me as a teenager was displayed at my 40th birthday party everyone kept asking me why we were featuring a picture of Jamie. But I just don't see it. And by not being able to recognize this very obvious and personal similarity I didn't think I would be a good judge of any possible resemblance to Nathan Mintz.

There was no doubt that I needed outside consultation on this one. So I found a picture of me at the same age as Nathan and posted them side by side so I could gather additional opinions.

My friends and family who examined the pictures split into three groups:

1. WOW. No question. Father and son.
2. There is a resemblance for sure, but hard to be definitive.
3. Just two Jewish kids from the Bronx.

Although there were some very strong opinions about the first and third choices, most of the votes went to the 'hard to be definitive' category. What do you think?

At this point in my quest, I considered this to be not much more than a parlor game. I playfully showed the pictures to anyone who had even the remotest interest in my story and tallied the opinions as they came in. As much fun as I was having with this, I didn't really give too much credence to the possibility that Nathan Mintz was indeed my biological father. This just seemed like a stab in the dark. Nevertheless, it was a whole lot more fun than just sitting around and waiting for possible DNA relatives to respond meaningfully to my messages.

Chapter 9

Barking Up Some Family Trees

I was intrigued enough by the photo similarity to continue my quest to see if I could either determine that Nathan Mintz was my biological father or conclusively rule it out.

To figure this out I leaned heavily on the tools offered on the Ancestry website. What made Ancestry so useful was that it was a triple threat. It combined DNA results, extensive historical records, and user-created family trees. So my next step was to find anyone on the site who had a public family tree that contained the name Nathan Mintz. Who knows, I just might hit the jackpot.

On June 28, I entered what I thought were very precise search terms into the Ancestry family tree search tool:

> First Name: Nathan
> Last Name: Mintz
> Birth Year: 1912
> Birth Place: New York City
> Death Year: 2001
> Death Place: New York City

It returned over 300,000 hits! What the hell? I was amazed that Ancestry even had that many family trees on their site, let alone having that many match my search specs. It didn't take long however to realize what was happening. Their default search parameters were quite broad. But the geek in me was also very impressed with this search tool. For example, when searching for the first or last name you could specify the match to be:

- Exact
- Similar
- Sounds Like
- Initials
- Broad

There were also similar specificity possibilities for the dates and locations. The reason I had so many matches was that the default search rule for First Name was 'Broad' while the rule for Last Name was 'Exact, Similar or Sounds Like'. When I restricted all of the parameters to be 'Exact' there was only one family tree that met these criteria. What a difference!

The sole tree returned was the Dershewitz/Rister family tree. It had hundreds of nodes across 5 generations. And sure enough, there was a node for Nathan Mintz. His entry in this tree seemed almost like an afterthought. He was included only because Nathan's brother Murray had married their family member Sylvia Dershewitz. The tree was managed by Sylvia's cousin Gene Dershewitz. So I sent him a message through Ancestry's messaging system with the subject line "Hoping You Can Help":

Hi Gene

I am trying to find information about Dr. Nathan Mintz (1912-2001) and noticed that he is tangentially included in your family tree. His brother Murray was married to your relative Sylvia Dershowitz.

Any information about either Nathan or Murray would be greatly appreciated. The most useful would be making contact with any living children or grandchildren of either man.

I am brand new to doing this type of research and don't really know the proper protocols. If what I am seeking is too intrusive or private, feel free to let anyone who might be willing to share to contact me here on Ancestry.

Let me know if you have any questions and thank you for your help.

All My Best

Joel Gottfried

While I wasn't quite as obsessed with getting his reply as I was with David Levine's, I nonetheless was really disappointed when I didn't quickly hear back from him. All I seemed to be doing on these DNA sites was sitting around and waiting for unknown but very intriguing people to message me.

Almost every day though, I received email notifications from one or more of the DNA companies that I had new matches to check out. Invariably these were 3rd cousins or even more distant relatives that I had decided wouldn't be fruitful avenues to explore.

On the morning of June 30 however, I saw a new listing that really got my heart racing. There was a young woman in her 20's named Jenna Kaufman on my list. Given her age and matching DNA (102 cm across 8 segments) she could have been as close as a 2nd cousin once removed, although it was just as likely that she also could have been a 3rd cousin or a great-niece or maybe even something more distant.

What really caught my attention about her information however was her family tree. In it, a man named Nathan Mintz was listed as one of her great grandfathers. If this bore out it could prove to be the missing link I was looking for. It is hard to overstate how excited I was at seeing this. I had just woken up and was exploring this on my iPad in bed before I even got my day started. My excitement was tempered somewhat when I investigated further. In particular, the Nathan Mintz shown on her tree had somewhat different birth and death years than my Nathan Mintz. In each case, they were only off by a few years. Though this would seem to indicate that this was a different person, the imprecision in much of genealogical research was such that this might actually prove to be a match.

Then I started to think through the logical implications of these purported relationships. If her Nathan Mintz was really my father and at the same time her great grandfather then there were only two possibilities. Either she was my granddaughter or my great-niece. For her to be my granddaughter then one of my two sons was her father. Yikes! If this were true it would be an even bigger mind-blowing genealogical discovery than George Gottfried not being my father! Besides the extraordinarily unlikely case that had happened without me knowing it, there was the matter of ages. David is only 12 years older than Jenna and Jamie just 10. While this might be biologically possible, this really didn't happen. Debbie's three sons are even younger than mine. So I wasn't her great uncle via Debbie's family either.

But what about my other potential half-siblings? I didn't know whether my Nathan Mintz had any children of his own or for that matter whether there were more donor inseminated half-siblings out there. My mind started to reel thinking about that one. Maybe I had several or dozens or even hundreds of other half-siblings. This was way too much to process at 6 AM! So I sent Jenna a message:

> Hi Jenna
>
> I am hoping you can help me find some information that has been puzzling in my search for my ancestors.
>
> According to Ancestry, we are 2nd or 3rd cousins. I have been trying to verify the identity of one of my possible relatives named Nathan Mintz. I noticed that there is someone with that name in your family tree as one of your great grandfathers.
>
> The Nathan Mintz I am looking for however has different birth and death dates (1912 - 2001) than the one you have listed. So my question is, how certain are you of the identity of the man you have listed (beyond the name)?
>
> It seems like quite a coincidence to be related to you and to both have a Nathan Mintz as an ancestor and have him not be the same person.
>
> Thank you so much for looking into this for me.
>
> Best
>
> Joel Gottfried
>
> PS Even if they are different people, it might be interesting to see where we do connect.

You'll never guess what happened next? That's right, I just waited for yet someone else not to respond. Was it me or was this just the nature of this type of research? Regardless, this was getting old and awfully frustrating.

Rather than sit on my hands I tried yet again. On July 5th I sent another Ancestry email to David Levine. On July 15th I tried again with Gene Dershewitz and Jenna Kaufman.

Both David and Jenna were incommunicado (what else is new?) but amazingly enough I heard back from Gene Dershewitz later that very same day:

> Joel,
>
> Sorry for not responding earlier. Just too much going on. If you send me your email address, I can forward it to my 2nd cousin, Maimoona Ahmed (formerly Myrna Mintz). Sylvia Dershowitz Mintz was her mother. Maimoona may have some personal recollections.
>
> Gene

Now we were getting somewhere. This was the first reply with a genuine possibility for connection. Maybe my luck had changed and my quest was now getting somewhere.

Chapter 10

Maimoona

On July 17, just two days later, I made email contact with Maimoona Ahmed. We quickly arranged a phone call for later that day. If Nathan Mintz was my biological father then Maimoona, as the daughter of Nathan's brother Murray, was my first cousin.

I prepared for the call by writing down a list of questions and thinking through how I wanted to broach the subject of the possibility that her uncle might be my father. I had no idea how close she had been with her uncle but the core of my questions and the very reason for my call was going to be a surprising and perhaps unwelcome assertion that her uncle, either in some professional or personal capacity, impregnated my mother.

I wanted to be careful how I did this so that she wouldn't be defensive and would be as receptive and forthcoming as possible. When the time for the call came I knew what I wanted to do but hadn't yet fully formulated exactly how I wanted to do it.

As it turns out, all this careful planning was for naught. From the first hello, Maimoona and I had an easy rapport with eager questions and candid information flowing in both directions. I didn't even have to raise the core question that I had so carefully thought through. Within a few minutes, she started musing about the possibility herself that we might be cousins. She was completely taken with the idea of a new close relative in her life.

Our entire conversation was inverted from what I expected. It started with her immediately zooming in on the underlying reason for the call and then only much later did we get to actually introduce ourselves and our families.

I learned that Maimoona was born in 1944 as Myrna Mintz. She attended college at Cornell University and received both BS and MS degrees in

Nutrition Sciences. She has traveled extensively studying the role that societies play in the nutrition of their people. While in college she met her eventual husband and chose to convert to Islam, his religion. She never liked her given name, which was inspired by the movie star Myrna Loy and changed it to Maimoona. She lives in California and is now a very active grandmother.

She provided quite a bit of information about her Uncle Nate and his family. As curious as I was about this it was way too much information provided way too soon and with a way too fast delivery for me to really absorb it all. Even now, I can barely make sense of the notes I took during the conversation. She told me numerous stories about the extended family. If I was sure that these people were in fact my family this would be very interesting. For now, however, it was definitely TMI. The whole notion that Nathan Mintz was my father was just based on some idle speculation and a possibly similar-looking picture.

There were a few things amidst all the information that stood out to me. This was a family of extremely well-educated and scientifically inclined people. And, by and large, they were noticeably taller than average compared to others in their generation. Hmmm. Just the traits that set me apart from my family. I put that into my 'Interesting Facts That Might Be Significant' folder to possibly revisit later.

She did tell me that her uncle had been married twice and had four children total from the two marriages. Three with his first wife Dorothy and one more with his second wife Edith.

She quickly agreed when I asked her if she would be willing to take a DNA test to see if we were related. She seemed to be as interested in this possibility as I was.

We were about to hang up when for some reason the conversation veered into descriptions of her paternal grandparents. These were the parents of her father and Uncle Nate. And of course, if all this played out as we were imagining, they were my grandparents too. I was ready to tune this out because once again while this seemed very interesting it was a bit too much too soon. During these descriptions, she let slip a very significant piece of information. Her grandmother Bessie's maiden name was Levine. I don't recall what prompted this revelation, but when I heard it I almost fell out of my chair. "You have got to be kidding me", I blurted out. I recounted to her how the most likely paternal relative who I was chasing online was also a Levine. This, more than anything else made me think I might be on the right track.

After hanging up with Maimoona I immediately ordered her a 23andMe DNA kit. In the ensuing days and weeks, while we were waiting for her DNA results, Maimoona kept sending me information about the family. There were names and descriptions of other relatives that she had previously neglected to tell me about. There were pictures and stories about ancestors from Russia. And most interesting of all were pictures and correspondences and detailed stories of Uncle Nate.

Looking through these was a unique experience for me. If this man was indeed my father I couldn't get enough of it. On the other hand, if this was a false alarm, as I still suspected it was, I was learning a ton about someone who delivered me into this world but otherwise had no bearing on my life.

Chapter 11

More Connections

While I was perusing all the information that Maimoona was sending me and also eagerly awaiting her DNA results, there was a major breakthrough back on the DNA front. I finally received the reports from the final two DNA testing companies that I had been waiting for (Family Tree and My Heritage).

The MyHeritage report had several interesting leads. A man who was almost certainly a 2nd cousin and then 3 or 4 more people who potentially were. Since neither Debbie nor the previously ubiquitous David Levine was on this site, I had no way of knowing which side of the family these potential relatives might be. So for the time being I added them to my 'Potential Paternal Cousins' file and figured I would come back to them when and if it made sense to do so.

The Family Tree report, on the other hand, had a very promising lead. My closest relative in their database was someone named Michael Levine. Yup, another Levine! His report didn't show how many segments we had in common, but it did show that we shared 216 cm of DNA. Family Tree estimated that we were either 2nd or 3rd cousins. My reading of the Shared CM chart indicated that he was most likely my 2nd cousin.

For no particularly good reason, I was sure that he was part of the same Levine family as David. After all, how many different Levine families could there be? And what are the chances that my top relative on two different DNA sites would each have the name Levine and be unrelated? It seemed like too big of a coincidence to be a random result.

But in my world view coincidences exist only so that they can be quantified. So I set out to see if I could make a reasonable guess at what the chances were that two random people whose last names were Levine would be closely related. I couldn't find any data to make that exact calculation but I did find some interesting results about the prevalence of Levines in the United States. Using Census Bureau data I found that there are slightly over 150,000 different last names in the US. And out of all those names, Levine ranks as the 926th most common. There are almost 41,000 people with the last name Levine. As a point of comparison, Gottfried is the 13,305th most common name with not quite 2,500 people. And for good measure, Mintz is the 5,428th most common name with almost 7,000 people. It is not surprising that Smith, Johnson, and Williams are the three most common surnames. I was also fascinated to find that Garcia, Rodriguez, and Martinez are also in the top ten. None of this was at all relevant to the quest to find my father, but it is very indicative of the type of numerical rabbit holes I can often descend.

While I couldn't quantify it, the higher than expected prevalence of Levines slightly dampened my enthusiasm that David and Michael were related. And on top of that, I found out from the same Census Bureau dataset that David is actually the most common first name among Levines and Michael is the second most common.

If Michael and David were related then Michael was also on my father's side of the family and would be a prime target of my research. If he was a cousin from my mother's side of the family, then I was decidedly less interested. While I was mulling over whether or not to reach out to him I found a very interesting way to resolve this question.

During my initial DNA research, I had learned about a public genealogy database and analysis site called GEDMatch. This site lets anyone who has already completed a DNA test at one of the commercial DNA testing companies to upload their information to this public site. Once uploaded it could then be compared with the DNA from anyone else who was also participating. It was a way to compare results from one DNA testing company to another. Or for that matter with any other source of DNA information that had made its way to the site.

I first learned about GEDMatch very early in my research process. This was when I was rather overwhelmed with the implications of all of this and was not yet knowledgeable about DNA testing. So it slipped through the cracks. I didn't even add it to my list of actions worth pursuing. In the back of my mind, I think I also minimized its usefulness. After all, I was already participating in all of the four major DNA companies. It didn't seem to me that I was very likely to find additional matches on GEDMatch that I wouldn't already know about.

Shortly after I dismissed GEDMatch as a research tool, it dramatically reappeared. In California, the police used it to solve a famous decade's long serial killer case called the 'Golden State Killer'. It was all over the news. According to Wikipedia:

> "The 'Golden State Killer' is a **serial killer**, rapist, and **burglar** who committed at least 13 murders, more than 50 **rapes**, and over 100 burglaries in **California** from 1974 to 1986. He is believed to be responsible for three crime sprees throughout California, each of which spawned a different nickname in the press before it became evident that they were committed by the same person."

The police took a copy of the perpetrator's DNA that they still had in one of the victim's rape kits and uploaded it to GEDMatch. Then just as I would use my DNA to find relatives they did the same with his. All told they found almost 20 relatives of interest. They then used the identities of these relatives along with standard genealogy tools to construct his likely family tree. The family tree pointed them to Joseph James DeAngelo, who immediately became their prime suspect. They acquired a sample of his DNA from some trash he discarded and found it was a perfect match to the original rape kit DNA. Case solved!

Besides the ingenuity of the detective work, this case raised lots of privacy questions for those of us who were analyzing and sharing our DNA. Each of the private companies has a carefully designed privacy setting to let you have some reasonable level of control over the availability of your results. However, once you uploaded your data to GEDMatch, all bets were off.

By its very nature, GEDMatch is a public database. While you can mask your identity by using an alias, it does require you to provide a valid email address so others can contact you. This is all explained when you first sign up for GEDMatch.

Once GEDMatch was reintroduced into my consciousness I decided to give it a try. Each of the testing companies has a utility to let you download your raw DNA results into a text file. I did this with each of them and then uploaded the raw data text files to GEDMatch. I knew that by using GEDMatch I was opening myself up for a more public and less controlled environment than I had with the private companies. However, this was during the period when my messages to possible relatives were going unanswered. I figured that anyone who I matched on GEDMatch, after having gone through the trouble of uploading their data and exposing their results to the public would be more motivated to correspond with me. And I really, really wanted to find out who my biological father was. Besides, I wasn't a serial killer and didn't have anything to hide.

Right after I uploaded my data it dawned on me that there was another very useful function that GEDMatch could serve. If I also uploaded Debbie's DNA then I would be able to immediately determine which side of the family any potential match was. I carefully explained the risks and rewards to Debbie and asked her if she was willing to do this. She said if it was OK by me it was OK by her.

So I set out to see what useful information I could glean from GEDMatch. You will never guess who was my closest match on the GEDMatch site? None other than Michael Levine. This time I could easily determine what side of the family he was on. He wasn't related to Debbie and thus became my prime target.

Chapter 12

The Levines

Now that I knew that Michael Levine was definitely related to me on my father's side and could well have been my 2nd cousin, I was ready to reach out to him. Unlike the other DNA testing companies, Family Tree does not have an internal messaging system. Instead, they provide the person's email address. It was clear from Michael's email address that it belonged to someone other than him. I had noticed when exploring the different DNA sites that this was not an uncommon occurrence. Sometimes a younger relative who was more technologically savvy would manage the account. On July 26 I sent my carefully worded introduction:

> Hi
>
> I am writing because Michael Levine shows up in my Family Tree DNA list as the closest relative to me and I would like to explore how we might be related.
>
> I am in an unusual situation. I am a 69-year-old man who has just learned through DNA testing that I don't know who my biological father is. I have some evidence to support the theory that there might be Levine's on this side of my family.
>
> I would be more than happy to discuss this in any fashion that is convenient for you.
>
> Thanks so much for your help.
>
> Best
>
> Joel Gottfried

The very next day I received just the reply I was hoping for:

Hi Joel-

I'm Michael Levine's daughter, Beth Levine Hammond. I've done a fair amount of work on our family tree with mixed results but I'm happy to help you if I can, with your interesting request! I forwarded your email to my dad (who's 84, but in pretty good physical/mental health), and he's happy to talk to you. I'd love to try figure out the connection- I'm more savvy with the computer/family tree info but he's got a memory like an elephant. Between both of us, I hope we can help you. You're welcome to contact me to discuss, and I can connect you with my dad: xxx-xxx-xxxx

Beth Levine Hammond

I had been at this for two full months. And this was the first time that I got such a timely and positive reply. And this was a two for the price of one special deal. Not only were they interested in talking to me but they had already done some genealogical research. I was super excited to see what my newfound cousins might know.

I swapped a couple of more emails with Beth. From my end, I filled her in on what I already knew (or at least thought that I knew). She was traveling for work and we made a plan to talk on the phone when she got back.

In the meantime, I gave Michael a call. He was a charming and gregarious man who was more than willing to tell me everything he knew about the family. And that was quite a lot. Not just his parents and grandparents, But siblings and cousins. He regaled me with family stories and marriages and divorces and health issues and relocations and more! Right now, I am looking at my notes from the call to remember all that he mentioned. My notes consist of a maze of names with boxes and arrows and asterisks. This was one active family! Despite all this, however, he had no recollection of Nathan Mintz's mother Bessie Levine being in the family.

Michael was an 84-year-old retired surgeon who lived in the Houston area. Given his age and the inherent ambiguity of the DNA testing, there was a possibility that he might be a 2nd cousin once removed rather than the 2nd cousin that the DNA seemed to indicate. I made a note to go back to the Family Tree DNA results to see if Beth was also in the database. If so, my DNA match with her might shed some light on my relationship with this part of the Levine family.

Amidst talk about all of the family connections, he told me something that really piqued my curiosity. He mentioned that I wasn't the first one to contact him with DNA evidence and an interesting story about a possible Levine family relationship. He said that I should talk to Dawn Bhat. She had been adopted and had done extensive DNA and genealogical research to find her biological family. This led her to discover that she too was part of the extended Levine clan. I made a very strong note to be sure to contact her.

The next day I called Beth and had another lovely chat. Just like it had been with Maimoona, I was struck by how easy it was to talk with both Michael and Beth. Although we were strangers to each other there was an openness to the conversation and a two-way willingness to share family information. I don't want to overstate the case, but it 'felt' like we were family.

Being such a data-oriented person, I am generally loathe to make sweeping generalities about groups of people. Notable exceptions for me to this rule is that I firmly believe that veterinarians and nurses are just a better class of people than the population at large. I was now thinking of adding amateur genealogists to the list!

Since I got so much family history from Michael my conversation with Beth was more focused on the process. She told me that through her genealogical research she was able to build a partial Levine family tree. She pointed me to the tree she had assembled and mentioned that one of the key pieces of information about our ancestors came from the 1910 census. I made a note to check that out for myself. And before we ended the conversation she made it a point to tell me that I should definitely talk to Dawn Bhat. Point taken!

My conversation with Beth was on Sunday, July 29. This was two days before I was going into the hospital for my stem cell transplant. I was expected to be in the hospital between 2 and 3 weeks. I couldn't decide whether the timing of all this new information with its needed follow-up activity was good or bad. I knew that I wasn't going to be as robust and energetic as I normally would be. On the other hand, this might be just the kind of distraction that I needed to keep me from fixating on how lousy I would be feeling. And I was definitely going to have a lot of free time on my hands!

I ordered a Bluetooth keyboard for my iPad so I could more efficiently use it for my genealogical pursuits and carefully assembled all of my notes and records to bring with me to the hospital. The next phase of this project was about to get underway.

Right before entering the hospital I carefully examined the Levine Family tree. It was quite comprehensive. There were almost 100 nodes across five generations of Levines. By my count, there were six additional living 2nd cousins who I could now contact. Even though none of these other potential 2nd cousins had had their DNA tested you never know what memories or insights or documents or even telling anecdotes they might have. I have watched enough TV police procedurals to know that it is often the seemingly small detail that blows the case wide open.

For now, what I wanted to focus on was who my direct ancestors might be. So I made a copy of the tree and ruthlessly trimmed from it all of the nodes that didn't help in that search. What was left I started calling the 'Potential Grandparent Tree' and looked like this:

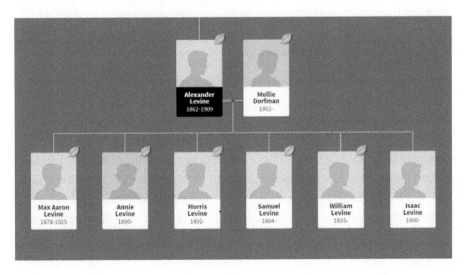

Going on the rather good assumption that Michael was my 2nd cousin, this tree now gave me the contours of my search. Namely that Alexander Levine and Molly Dorfman were my great grandparents. That meant that one of their (at least) 6 children was a grandparent of mine. I also realized I even knew a bit more than that. Of these 6 children, I could rule out Michael's grandfather, Max Aaron. After all, if he was also my grandfather then Michael and I would be 1st cousins. However, the amount of DNA we shared was well less than even the lower bound found for 1st cousins. That left the other five people to explore. If my calculations were correct, one of them had a male child who was my father.

I kept staring at the tree hoping that this concentrated mental energy would somehow produce results. While there weren't any miracles in the offing I did notice something odd. Take a look at the birth years of their children:

Max Aaron	1878
Annie	1890
Morris	1892
Samuel	1894
William	1895
Isaac	1900

While anything is possible, it seemed unlikely to me that Alexander and Mollie would wait 12 years between their first two children and then start popping them out every couple of years. So I remained open to the fact that there might be some missing children between Max Aaron and Annie and hence more potential grandparents for me to consider.

To get a better handle on this I decided to check out the 1910 census for myself. According to the census records, Alexander (who had died in 1909) and Mollie had immigrated to the US from Russia with their children in 1906. In 1910 Mollie was living on the lower east side in Manhattan with six children, one daughter-in-law, and three grandchildren. But the census record also indicates that Mollie had eight living children, not six. So it sure seemed that my supposition about the missing children was very likely correct. Who were the missing two children? Yet more questions and even more importantly more potential grandparents.

By the way, I say 'likely' rather than 'surely' because the census information itself is sometimes inaccurate or hard to interpret. Take a look at the actual 1910 census record for Mollie and her clan. How sure would you be that everything you see and are trying to understand is correct?

While examining the census record I couldn't help but wonder what life was like for this family. There were 11 people of all ages crammed into one small (at least in my imagination) apartment. According to the census, Mollie and her oldest child Max Aaron only spoke Yiddish. Except for Isaac, the youngest child, none of the children had attended school. When I zoomed out I saw that all of their neighbors were in similar situations. As I had when doing my research on Grandma Gussie and her family I was already feeling a connection with these people.

Given the likelihood of two additional children and the certainty that Max Aaron was not my grandfather I updated the Potential Grandparent Tree accordingly:

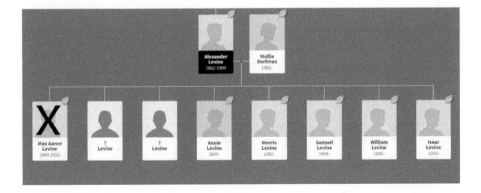

Even though I had just added two new possible grandparents while only eliminating one, this felt like real progress. As Chairman Mao once said while preaching patience, "One step forward, two steps backward". OK, OK.....I know it was really "One step backward, two steps forward" but this still felt like I was getting somewhere.

At this point, I was becoming increasingly optimistic that I would eventually find my father. I had the framework for where to look and leads to follow up on to fill in that framework. And there was also Maimoona's pending DNA results which just might prove conclusive.

Chapter 13

Dawn Bhat

As soon as I finished my call with Beth Hammond I went to see if Dawn Bhat showed up as a relative in any of the DNA sites. I found her in the FamilyTree database and she was indeed listed as a relative of mine. It indicated that we shared 125 cm of DNA and were likely to be 2nd to 4th cousins. According to Michael and Beth, Dawn was younger than me so was probably not a direct cousin. And sure enough the Shared CM Project relationship chart showed that she was most likely a 2nd cousin once removed.

This had been one of my targeted relationships. So why had I not noticed her? Because according to FamilyTree there were 215 other people in their database who were more closely related to me than Dawn. There is no way I would have worked my way that far down the list. So, if I had missed Dawn, how many other Levine relatives had I also overlooked? This did make me realize what a big job this could be. To be thorough about it I would have to pre-screen each person to see if they were even on my father's side of the family. This is something I could only do on sites where I had Debbie's DNA. This seemed like a lot of work, so I added it to my 'Try This If I'm Desperate' file for possible future reference.

It was getting late on Sunday night and I was heading into the hospital the next day, so I immediately sent Dawn an email:

Hi Dawn

I am writing because your DNA showed as a match with mine and I would really like to explore how we might be related.

I have just spoken with Michael Levine and Beth Levine Hammond about my possible relationship with them. I understand from them that you too have recently found out that you are also part of their family.

I am in an unusual situation. I am a 69-year-old man who has just learned through DNA testing that I don't know who my biological father is. I have some evidence to support the theory that there might be Levine's on this side of my family.

I would be more than happy to discuss this in any fashion that is convenient for you.

Thanks so much for your help.

Best

Joel Gottfried

In keeping with my current string of quick and positive communications, Dawn replied to me in less than an hour:

Hi Joel,

Yes, I would be happy to talk with you! Beth and her dad are distant relatives of mine but have been absolutely wonderfully supportive in my personal search. They have the most detailed Levine tree I am aware of, which I imagine Beth gave you access to as well. As I did, you may figure out how you fit in this DNA family tree. I am in touch with my relatives from the Levine family and would be glad to share any info that might help with your search.

Please give me your number and when may be a good time to reach you.

Where are you from? My Levine relatives are mostly from NY.

Warmly,
Dawn

We swapped a few more emails before setting up a time to chat. With my impending hospital stay, I didn't have a sense of how I would be feeling and what my schedule would be. As it turned out day 2 was completely an off day. This was the day when all I was doing was waiting for the chemo to clear my system so that the stem cells could be safely added. This early on I wasn't yet feeling its bad effects. The nurses told me that I was free to leave the hospital to walk around the neighborhood or go out to dinner or pretty much whatever else I might feel like. Debbie and my friends Carl and Dru were visiting, so we went to a casual but lovely restaurant for what I was calling my 'Last Supper'. It was during this meal that Dawn called. I excused myself and went out to the restaurant's patio to take the call.

I learned from Dawn that she had been adopted at birth in a secretive private market adoption transaction. Her adoptive parents kept this a complete secret from her. She had a younger sister just 13 months younger than her who entered the family the natural way. She commented that she felt that she stood out in her family because she was academically very advanced in a family that wasn't and was notably shorter than the rest of them. These differences were just like mine (except I was noticeably taller). Also while she was noticing this as a child I hadn't given my situation a second thought.

When she was in her 30's an odd incident triggered her to question whether she might be adopted. Her mom's gynecologist had just been released from prison. There were rumors that he had committed insurance fraud and might also have been using his own sperm as part of fertility treatments (sound familiar?). What was odd was that her mom was in regular contact with him. She shared this with a friend who offhandedly remarked that maybe the doctor is really her father. While this comment came out of left field it sparked just enough questioning in her to start to investigate.

She went to the hospital that she had been told was where she was born and there was no record of her birth there. A visit to her former pediatrician confirmed that she was in fact adopted. After that, she took advantage of New York's adoption information laws. These allow adopted children to receive non-identifying information about their birth mother. In her case, she now knew that her mother was Jewish and 25 years old when Dawn was born. This was 2006 and while DNA testing was possible it was very expensive and not yet a readily available consumer product.

In 2013, after the birth of her own daughter, she decided to renew her search by having her DNA analyzed. Just like I was doing she started following the leads as they presented themselves. And just as I did she got a major assist from Beth Hammond who helped connect her to the Levine family. With a little more digging she found out who her biological mom and dad were. Her mom was the one who was part of the Levine family. She continued to gather information and build her family tree.

What was key for me in all this information was that her mom's grandfather was William Levine, who was one of Alexander and Mollie's children. Since our shared DNA indicated that Dawn and I were most likely 2nd cousins once removed, that meant that her mom was my 2nd cousin and William Levine was my great uncle. More importantly, he wasn't my grandfather. I wasted no time in updating the potential grandparent family tree:

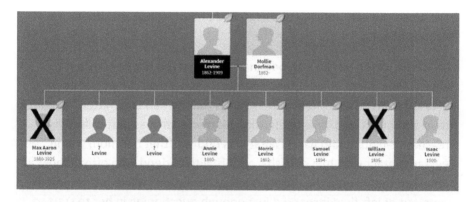

In addition to all this information, Dawn put me in touch with Priscilla Sharp. Priscilla is an experienced genealogist, advocate for adoptee rights, and a self-proclaimed 'Search Angel'. She offers free services to those (primarily adoptees) who need help finding their biological roots. I emailed her with the details of my situation. Given her professional expertise, I went into great detail even including the shared cm of each possible match. She got back to me with confirmation about my approach but also a warning.

> You are on the right track as far as the Levine family is concerned. Except one thing you should keep in mind. Endogamy in small European Jewish communities over the years has led to overlapping chromosomes in modern generations giving the appearance of a relationship closer

than actual. For example, your Levine cousins might actually be 3rd, not 2nd, so you'll want to go back another generation and doing so, might actually find the connection with the doctor.

I duly noted this caveat, but it still hit me that it was more likely that I was only three generations removed from Alexander and Mollie rather than four. It went beyond the DNA evidence from Michael and Dawn that indicated this. If I was four generations removed from Alexander and Mollie, then the average age of parenthood at each generation would have been 18 years old. Possible but less likely than the 22 year average age of three generations. While understanding that it was not an ironclad fact, I did proceed on the assumption that everything was as it appeared to be. Alexander and Mollie were my great grandparents, Michael was my 2nd cousin and Beth and Dawn were 2nd cousins once removed.

Chapter 14

David Levine Again

After the euphoria of my big breakthroughs with Beth, Michael, and Dawn things slowed down. As best I could I kept scouring the DNA results for possible leads but found only low likelihood options. On top of that, the results of the chemotherapy and my absent immune system had finally kicked in. I felt like crap. The best antidote to this was to try and keep busy. And the best way to keep busy was to work on my genealogical fatherhood project.

So, on August 10 I decided that my best bet was to reach out to David Levine one more time:

> Hi Again David
>
> Would love to see your family tree. I have unearthed some evidence that I might belong in it.
>
> Thanks again
>
> Joel Gottfried

Amazingly he replied the next day.

> I can't give you access because it is not my tree. It was started by J Wertheim. I'm not sure how to contact him other than through ancestry.com

This was disappointing but the very quick reply was encouraging. So I immediately replied.

Thanks for the info. I will try and reach out to him/her myself.

I was hoping the tree would clarify some intriguing possibilities for me. I am searching for my biological father and I think you might have the key to unlocking this mystery for me. You are by far the closest DNA relative of mine out here (with the exception of my half-sister). And since you are unrelated to her, you must be on my father's side. I have found some other Levine's that are also close relatives.

Would you be willing to communicate directly so we can see what the connection really is? If so, you can reach out to me via email at xxxx.com

Hope to hear from you soon.

Joel Gottfried

After all this time I had finally established meaningful contact with David. The next day he replied and offered to give me a call to discuss our family. I was thrilled. I sent him an email with my phone number and a complete description of all I knew so far. I figured that would help structure our discussion. The next day (August 13) he gave me a call. As with all of the other family members I had spoken with, this too was a delightful conversation. He was 62 years old, living in Connecticut and like Michael, was also a retired surgeon (what is it with doctors in this family?).

By the way, as a child, I always said that I too wanted to become a doctor. This lasted long enough and seemed serious enough that when I reached junior high school and had to decide on a foreign language, my mom recommended that I take Spanish. Her reasoning was that would facilitate my communications with any Hispanic patients I might have. When I reached high school I realized that math and physics were much more interesting to me than biology and chemistry. So I abandoned my nascent medical career and spared any possible Hispanic patients my rather weak grasp of Spanish.

Despite the lengthy delay and several false starts in making contact with David, he was very forthcoming with family information and had lots of memories about the Levine family.

Our call was a bit constrained from my end, however. By this time, my immune system had just started to re-establish itself. Although I was feeling just a bit better than I had at the nadir of this terrible experience I was still far from normal. I couldn't fully focus nor easily connect all of the family threads he was explaining to me. Amazingly though I felt comfortable enough to share all of this with David. This is not something that I would normally tell a stranger. But it felt natural with him. He shared comparable information about himself and that just helped to bring us closer.

I was hoping that David would be able to identify his grandfather for me so that I could update my grandparent tree. He didn't disappoint with that, though the story had a twist. In the 1910 census, Mollie's youngest child was listed as Isaac. David told me that his name in Russia was the equivalent of Israel. In the US he became Isaac. He wanted something more Americanized and began calling himself Irving and that stuck. With this confirmation, I updated the potential grandparent tree accordingly.

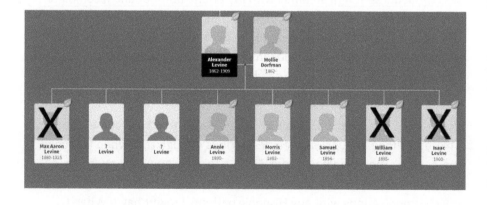

But David wasn't done yet! In the biggest development I had yet uncovered, he told me that he was well acquainted with Nathan Mintz. He referred to him as 'cousin Nat'. This could well be the big breakthrough I had been looking for. Nathan was his father's first cousin and the two families were very close. His family lived on Long Island but he remembers visiting Nathan in what seemed to him to be a very upscale apartment in a very upscale part of Manhattan. His father Jules was Nathan's accountant and Nathan was his mom's OB/GYN. In fact cousin Nat delivered David and his brother at Doctor's Hospital. He said that Nathan was loved by everyone.

Though the tough hospital stay had taken its toll on my mental acuity, it didn't take much to realize what I had just heard. If Nathan Mintz was my father and he was David's dad's first cousin then David and I would be 2nd cousins. This is exactly what our DNA results predicted. This didn't prove that Nathan Mintz was my biological father. But his being my father was now perfectly consistent with the available data. Considering him to be my father was no longer just a speculative guess that was devoid of data. My two lines of inquiry had now merged into one data-driven one. This pleased the data geek in me no end. I now considered it substantially more likely that Nathan Mintz was my biological father than he wasn't.

There was still the niggling question of where Nathan's mom Bessie fit into all this. The only thing that made sense was that she was one of Mollie's two missing children. If this were the case then it would also explain how I was also related to Michael, Beth, and Dawn. So I set out to see if I could fill this hole too.

Using the search tools on Ancestry I found the marriage license for Bessie Levine and Louis Mintz that was dated May 26, 1907. That meant that by the 1910 census Bessie was already married and could well have been living with Louis in their own household. So I checked the 1910 census for them and indeed found them living in their own place with their three-year-old son Moses. The age of Moses corresponds exactly to that of Nathan's older brother Murray. So once again a Jewish name later became Americanized. There was now a very good chance that Bessie was one of the two missing children.

I might have been jumping the gun just a bit, but I updated the 'Potential Grandparent Tree' to be the "Is He My Biological Father Tree'.

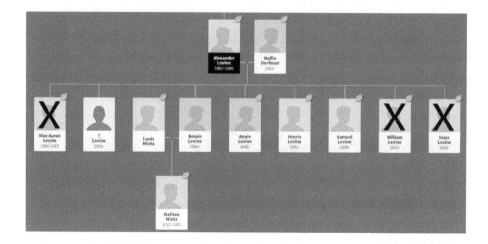

As useful as these family trees were to help me make sense of the relationships, there is nothing quite as good as a picture of those involved. Maimoona found a picture of the Levine clan that seems to have been taken on the occasion of Bessie's engagement to Louis Mintz.

Levine family with Louis Mintz circa 1907

No one I have contacted knows for sure who each person in the picture is. But by comparing the pictures of the people with the ages in the family tree I think it is pretty clear who we are looking at. Louis is sitting at the extreme right with his fiancé Bessie resting her (fisted!) hand on his shoulder. Bessie's mom Mollie is seated in the center. I am guessing that the young woman at the extreme left is the missing child in my family tree, who to this day has escaped my discovery. To her left (and our right) is either Morris or Samuel. Over Mollie's left shoulder is Annie. Seated in the front row would be William and the youngest sibling standing to Mollie's left is Irving: One thing that struck me immediately when I saw this picture, is that with the possible exception of the toddler Irving, no one is smiling. That might have just been the way posed pictures were in those days or this might not have been the happiest of families. And who poses for her engagement photo with a dour expression and a clenched fist?

In addition to the key information about the Levine family that seemingly cracked this mystery wide open, David also had some intriguing nuggets about the Mintz side of the family. The day after our conversation he forwarded me an email he received from the administrator of something called the 'Mintz Family Project'. Who knew such a thing even existed! This is a group that is trying to build the complete family tree of all those who have descended from Yerachmiel (Robert) Mintz who arrived in New York City in 1870. If Nathan Mintz was my father and he was a descendant of Robert Mintz then this would be the ideal way to gather information about my father's paternal relatives. So far I had only been focusing on his maternal ancestors, the Levines. As fascinating as this was I put it aside for three reasons.

First and foremost I didn't need it to find out if Nathan Mintz was my father. Maimoona's DNA results, when available, would answer that question. Second, it required a different type of DNA test. All of my searching so far was based on what is called an autosomal DNA test. The Mintz group was using Y-DNA testing. This traces ancestry strictly through male lineage. I was happy with my progress and didn't see the need for another round of DNA testing. And finally, there was no guarantee that he even was a descendent of Robert Mintz anyway.

With David's useful and tantalizing information in hand, I was now waiting for two big events: leaving the hospital and getting Maimoona's DNA results.

Chapter 15

The Big Reveal

They kept telling me in the hospital that my immune system numbers had to rise to a certain level before I could go home. They were disappointedly just inching up. It looked like I would be there a while longer. But amazingly, as soon as I spoke with David Levine, my numbers rose dramatically. I am not suggesting that this was a cause and effect relationship, but there was no mistaking that with potentially very good news on one front I also had very good news on the other front.

My departure from the hospital on August 15, just 2 days after speaking with David was not uneventful. In the hospital, because I had such a limited immune system, I had been on prophylactic antibiotics. That didn't stop me from contracting pneumonia. Another antibiotic was administered intravenously to combat that. Shortly after getting home, I was diagnosed with an infection from the Clostridium difficile bacterium. This is more commonly referred to as C. diff and can be quite serious. For me, it manifested itself as non-stop diarrhea. Ironically, the typical cause of C. diff is having been treated with too many antibiotics. These wind up stripping your system of good bacteria. This in turn allows the C. diff to thrive. Yet one more antibiotic and a bit more than a week of time cleared this up. Needless to say, it was hard to focus on my search under these circumstances.

As luck would have it, as soon as the C. Diff disappeared on August 25th I got word from Maimoona that her DNA results were posted on the 23andMe site. We set up a call for later that day to review them. This was the first day that my innards were feeling normal. The gastrointestinal rumblings were now replaced with nervous energy. Maimoona had several family obligations and couldn't call until early that evening. Because she was in California this wasn't so early for me. As I had been anxiously awaiting to hear these results, I would have taken this call at any time day or night.

While we were on the phone I talked her through the necessary steps to share her results with me. Within just a few minutes she did that. When I refreshed my screen, there she was. Second on my list of DNA relatives, right after Debbie. According to 23andMe we shared 12.1% of our DNA. I dug deeper and saw that we had 902 cm of DNA in common across 27 segments. I didn't need to look this up in the cm table or even take a look at what 23andMe predicted our relationship was. It was crystal clear to me that we were 1st cousins. It was now definitively determined that Nathan Mintz was my father.

This was exactly three months to the day after Debbie and I had made our initial shocking discovery. At first, the significance of this didn't fully sink in. I didn't feel elated that I now knew the truth. I was actually a bit stunned by the sudden definitiveness of it. This had been such a huge focus of my life for the last three months and now it had abruptly ended.

Maimoona and I continued to talk about what it was like to officially become close relatives in such an unconventional way. We talked a bit about Nathan's children who were now confirmed as my half-siblings. And we finally came up with a plan to stay in touch and see how our relationship might evolve.

It was fairly late at night when the conversation ended. I quickly went into our bedroom where Susan was already in bed, but not quite asleep yet. I sat somewhat dazedly on the recliner in the corner of the bedroom and said, "It's confirmed. Nathan Mintz is my father". She replied, "Well then, you have Nathan Mintz to thank for your intelligence."

At that moment the significance of this really sunk in. Up until then, this whole process was primarily a detective mystery. A puzzle where I was trying to find the right name to put into a missing box in a family tree. It was an exciting and motivating pursuit because it was personal, but it was nonetheless mainly an intellectual challenge.

But now it felt different. I was who I am to a large extent because this stranger was my father. If George and Tina had had a baby boy named Joel who was born at the exact same time as I was but who was conceived in the normal way, he wouldn't be me. I was someone other than just their son. Of course, I was the son they raised, and decades of growing up and living with them had a profound effect on me. But at that moment I could feel the 'nature' part of the nature vs. nurture debate asserting itself. I felt like an outsider looking in at my family of origin. Who exactly was I?

I sat on that chair for quite a while wrestling with this. As Susan fell asleep her words kept running through my head. When I first learned that I wasn't George's son it was a shock. Like a bolt of lightning. Powerful in its impact but brief in its duration. This was more like a flood. Slow in developing but much more persistent in its effect.

I couldn't stop asking myself, "Who am I?" over and over again as I sat there. What were the most salient aspects of my inner self? The ones that really defined who I was. I could enumerate several that I treasured, but the one that I couldn't shake loose was my analytical outlook on almost everything I encountered. It permeated my sense of the world. It was the way I interacted with everyone and everything. It was me! And it clearly came from Nathan Mintz.

In the following days, I recounted my experience with Maimoona to my boys and Debbie, and then my friends. The telling and retelling of the story helped to make it seem more real. Of course, this is who I was. How could it possibly be anything other than this? With time, I regained my life balance, albeit with a new equilibrium.

Chapter 16

My New Family

The new equilibrium of my life extended beyond just coming to grips with my personal heritage. At the age of 69, I had unexpectedly acquired a brand new family. This raised all sorts of questions. Who were these people? Besides the very close biological relationships we shared, would or could we have anything meaningful between us? Was I interested in exploring with them what this could mean? Would they be interested?

To this point, I had had nothing but positive and welcoming interactions with Maimoona and my Levine 2nd cousins who had been so generous in sharing family and personal information with me. In December 2019 I was in California visiting my family and decided to take the opportunity to visit Maimoona. We spent much of a full day together catching up on a lifetime of missed connections. As it had been on the phone, she was easy to be with and I felt a genuine connection. I am looking forward to seeing where this and these other relationships might lead.

Maimoona told me that Nathan had been married twice and had three children with his first wife and one more with his second wife. And on top of that, Nathan's sister Gertrude had two boys, who were also my first cousins.

Technically my newfound half-siblings were genetically as close to me as Debbie. Clearly whatever relationship I might develop with any of them, it would never come close to what Debbie and I have built over a lifetime. Nevertheless, I was rather intrigued and wanted to find them to see if we could connect.

There were two half-brothers (Max and Alan) and two half-sisters (Sandra and Rachel). Rachel was from the second marriage and was younger than me, while the other three were all older. Maimoona had lost touch with them and had only very limited information about how to find them.

Of the four it looked like it would be the easiest to find Max Mintz. Maimoona knew that he was born in 1942 and was fairly certain that he was a college professor. If that were so he would most likely have a semi-public presence and be easy to find and contact. A quick Google search didn't disappoint. Not only was he a college professor, but amazingly enough he also lived in Philadelphia and was in the computer science department at the University Of Pennsylvania. He has been at Penn since 1974. I was a graduate student and a Research Professor at Penn from 1979 to 1984. While I wasn't in the computer science department we were both in the Engineering School at the same time. Might we have crossed paths?

As a current professor, there was a ton of information about his interests, activities, and how to reach him. There was even a brief 'documentary' about him. It was a five-minute video from 2011 that introduced him and gave him a chance to speak about his teaching interests and philosophy. I watched it several times. We didn't look at all alike (but then again what do I know?). But his teaching philosophy and mannerisms were very similar to those that animated my outlook when I was teaching.

Not only the content, but the phraseology sounded incredibly familiar to me. At one point, decrying the focus on grades vs. learning he said, "I would if I could, give you your degree as soon as you get here so that we could get down to the serious business of education". I had chills down my spine when I heard that. Many years ago when I was teaching at an alternative high school we were having a vigorous debate in a faculty meeting about grades. The point I made in that debate was the same one Max was making and astoundingly with almost those exact words.

I decided to reach out to Max and see if he might be interested in exploring this rather amazing connection. I thought the easiest way to do so was via email. But I really struggled with how to word this introductory message so that it didn't sound like I was a Nigerian prince. I wrote and discarded draft after draft. Not only was it difficult to set the right tone but I realized as I was doing this that I was a bit nervous about contacting him. This was the first time in the whole process where I felt this way. I think it is because of the closeness of our biology and the possibility of something and someone so close being added to my life.

Susan is a professional marketer and a pro at using words effectively. So I enlisted her to edit my email. We tried our best to write something that reduced the chance that he would think this was a scam and at the same time try to pique his curiosity about me. To this date, I am not completely convinced that we succeeded. But on August 27 I sent Max the following email at his UPenn address with the subject 'Family DNA Connection':

> Hi Max
>
> I know this message is coming to you out of the blue, but I have recently discovered that my biological father is actually your dad, Nathan Mintz. I am reaching out to you to possibly explore this incredible connection.
>
> Let me introduce myself. My name is Joel Gottfried, and I am a 69 year old retired grandfather who lives in the Chestnut Hill area of Philadelphia. I have an engineering PhD from Penn and spent the largest part of my career developing advanced interactive data analysis software for the survey research industry.
>
> A few months ago my sister gave me a 23andMe DNA kit for my birthday and got one for herself. We were both utterly shocked when the results showed we were only half-siblings. From that point on I began my quest to find out who my biological father and missing family might be. I used traditional genealogical tools and DNA results to piece together my ancestry. I would be happy to share the details with you if you are interested.
>
> I am sure you are stunned by this news. I do know what that feeling is like!
>
> At this point, I would love to correspond and possibly meet if you are so inclined. I leave it to you to decide whatever approach is most comfortable for you. If you are not interested in exploring this any further, I would be disappointed but would completely respect your decision and privacy.
>
> Best
>
> Joel Gottfried

I nervously awaited his reply. But none was forthcoming. On September 4 I re-sent the message. Once again I waited and waited and waited. No reply whatsoever. There was a very small chance that my messages had been treated as spam (hello Nigerian princes!) so Susan came up with a slightly different strategy to reach him.

As if all the connections with Max weren't enough, there was one more. Susan is the Director of Marketing at the Morris Arboretum, which is part of the University Of Pennsylvania. She suggested that it might be better if she reached out to him. Besides being a slightly different angle on approaching him the email would be coming from one UPenn email address to another and definitely wouldn't be flagged as spam. On October 18, Susan sent him a message with the subject 'Amazing Coincidence' that included my original message but led off with:

> Hi Max
>
> My name is Susan Crane and I work at the Morris Arboretum, which is actually part of UPenn.
>
> My husband, Joel Gottfried, has sent you a couple of emails about an amazing family connection with you that he has recently discovered. I am following up on the off chance that his emails went to spam and you never received them.
>
> As you can see in his original message, which I have copied below, he is genuinely interested in getting in touch with you about this connection.
>
> Thanks for considering his request.
>
> Best
>
> Susan Crane

Once again we waited and waited, but to this date have never heard back from him. This is a huge disappointment. I am convinced that he has received these messages and is consciously choosing not to acknowledge my existence. I'm not sure whether he thinks there might be some kind of scam going on or if he knows the emails are legitimate but just doesn't want to open up what could be a difficult new chapter in his life. And there is even the possibility that I might not even be the first person to approach him with news like this.

A while after sending these messages I have thought about trying to find someone who we might know in common to approach him. This would definitely eliminate the scam possibility and maybe the personal touch would sway him to respond. With just a little bit of digging, I found several possible candidates who might fit the bill. But, I have decided to honor my original message to him, where I said that I would respect his desire to not engage with me.

Susan trying to construct the perfect anti-scam message

While it was very easy to find Max, I was having difficulty finding my other three half-siblings. As I was trying to figure out a more effective way to find them I realized I had another possibility. Maimoona had mentioned that Nathan's younger sister Gertrude (who she referred to as Goldie) had two sons, Bill and Bob Berkowitz. Though she had also lost touch with them, she did have enough information to enable me to proceed. She knew that Bill had passed away and that Bob would be easy to find. Bob used to be a general news reporter for ABC News, a men's correspondent for the Today Show, and the CNN White House correspondent. He currently provides communications consulting services. On October 18, I reached out to Bob via email introducing myself as his first cousin and the rather unusual circumstances that led me to this discovery. He wrote back immediately and was eager to learn more. We spoke on the phone later that day. As stunned as he was by this completely out of the blue message, he was able to easily shift into reporter mode and just gobble up the information I had.

In addition to getting to know him, I had an ulterior motive in making contact. I was hoping that, unlike Maimoona, he hadn't lost contact with my siblings. There was good news and bad news on this front. He had in fact not been in touch with the three older ones but indicated he was fairly close with Rachel. He went so far as to send her an email about me while we were talking. And he also heard back from her during our conversation. Other than indicating that she was also stunned he didn't reveal anything else about her. After not hearing from Rachel after this I emailed Bob a few weeks later asking him to pass along another message from me to Rachel. So far, just like with Max, I have not heard anything at all from her.

As I prepared to write this book I decided to try one more time to find Sandra, Alan, and even Rachel. With a fresh mind and a more organized approach, I found success on all three fronts.

Ironically it can be harder to gather information about more recent relatives than older ones. One of the primary sources of information is the US Census database. However, there is a law that all Census data be kept strictly private for 72 years from the date of the census. That means that nothing more recent than the 1940 census is available. Since my older siblings were born in the 1940s this wouldn't do me any good. They wouldn't show up until the 1950 census is made available in 2022.

Sandra was born in 1941 and is currently 80 years old. I found her high school yearbook picture (don't even ask if she looks like me!). Maimoona had told me that she was 5' 11" tall and had done some professional modeling as a young woman. In her class photo, she is in the middle row of students with all her female classmates. What is noteworthy is that she is easily a head taller than all of them.

After this quick success, I hit a stone wall. I couldn't find any personal or professional information about her life. Ultimately I did find some current information about her. But even this was limited, just her address and landline telephone number. With email not a possibility I contacted her the old-fashioned way, by US Mail. On April 23, 2019, I sent her a letter very similar to the email I had sent Max. Even though that one didn't work and might even have seemed a bit like a scam, I just couldn't figure out a better way to communicate my story. I did indicate in the letter that this wasn't a scam (but that is just what a scammer would say!) and I provided every possible way for her to contact me. So far, as with the others, absolutely no contact from her.

When I sharpened my focus on Rachel I was able to find out quite a bit. I learned that she is a music producer who lives in Manhattan. I found promotional photos as well as pictures from music events such as South By Southwest. With this information, I was able to get her address, email, and phone numbers. Since she had already heard from me through Bob and elected not to reply I have decided to honor my previous promise not to intrude any further into her privacy.

Having struck out with the other three, I set out to look for Alan. I started my search for Alan not even sure how to spell his name. Alan? Allen? Allan? Since my middle name is Alan I decided to start there. All I knew from Maimoona was that he was born in 1946 or 1947. I quickly found two different birth records for an Alan Mintz in New York in that time period that were separated by just 3 months. One was in late 1946 and the other in early 1947. I set out to follow each one and see what I could find.

Soon enough it was clear which one was the correct one. I had noticed when researching Max that his middle name is Luria. This was his mother's maiden name. I found the Social Security Administration death record for an Alan Luria Mintz that matched one of the two birth records. In addition to that, I also discovered that this Alan Mintz was buried in the same cemetery as Dorothy Luria. This was Nathan's first wife and would have been Alan's mother. This had to be him.

I was so used to researching long past ancestor information that at first it didn't hit me as odd that he had already passed away. But he wasn't an ancient ancestor. He was my half-brother. He was my contemporary, just a bit more than 2 years older than me. He was only 58 when he died in 2004.

I began to wonder what his relatively brief life must have been like. It didn't take too much more digging to find out that he had been a veteran. He had joined the Army in September 1965 and was discharged in May 1966. This was odd on several fronts. First was the duration of the service. He only served for 8 months, which was way shorter than what it would typically be for either a draftee or an enlistee. I didn't find his discharge papers, so I don't know what the circumstances of his discharge were. But they were certainly an exception to the normal course of events. Also, this was at the height of the Vietnam War. Over a quarter of a million young men were drafted in 1965. However, very few of them were children of privilege, as Alan surely was. In those days there were local draft boards that determined each draftee's status. A son of a wealthy local physician almost always found a way out (bone spurs anyone?). Of course, he might have enlisted or otherwise chosen not to contest his draft status. But this too would have been unusual for a wealthy New York Jewish boy.

Alan's life had a very different trajectory than those of his father and older brother. They both had immense academic successes and long and distinguished careers. Why had Alan taken such a different path? Why had he joined the Army as an 18-year-old? Why had he only lasted 8 months? What led to his death at age 58? Lots of unanswered questions. And so far, I haven't been able to figure out any of the answers to these questions. Neither Maimoona nor Bob knew what had happened to Alan. I assume Max would know, but so far that is also out of my reach.

Despite the dearth of information about Alan, I kept imagining that he had a rough life. His brief Army tour and his early death made me think that he could have been beset with either health issues or other life problems. While this, quite clearly, is pure speculation on my part, I was drawn to it by the parallels it drew with my younger brother Stuart.

Like Alan, Stuart joined the military. And like Alan, he died young (age 48). Stuart struggled throughout his brief life to find his way. He had difficulty finding and holding jobs and always seemed to be in some kind of emergency. My dad had to repeatedly bail him out of different types of jams and at one point helped him declare bankruptcy to get a fresh start.

After my dad died, Stuart leaned on me for help. In the 1980's I worked for a company that had a toll-free 800 number. Back in those days of very expensive long-distance phone calls that was indeed a big deal. He took advantage of this to call me from Florida virtually every day. He had lots to say based on lots of misconceptions about lots of topics. It took quite a bit of restraint not to yell, "What the hell are you talking about!" every time he called. He was a one-man precursor to Fox News! I mostly let him have his say since I sensed that he really didn't have a chance to pontificate like this anywhere else.

In 2007, just a few months after my mother died, Stuart succumbed to prostate cancer. As much a pain in the ass as he was I really do miss him. Being 10 years older than him, and especially after my dad died, I was as much a parent as an older brother. Like I do with my grandparents, I make it a point to visit him every year. Every winter I make a brief trip to Florida that includes a visit to the National Cemetery there to re-connect with him. In the era of Trump I can only imagine what I would be hearing from him were he still alive.

Unfortunately, it is likely that I will never hear from any of my Mintz siblings. I am not even expecting a "not interested" note. Why that is I can't be sure. On a practical level, I am now missing important family health history that might advise my medical care. But more importantly, it is a shame that this part of my background and being is shut off to me. I had a vision of making new connections with at least some of them and of gaining additional insight into who I am and where I came from.

It is only fitting that my inability to connect with them has heightened my awareness and appreciation of my original and existing family. And for that matter on the nature of family itself. After my mother and Stuart had died I mentioned to Debbie, "I guess the family is just us now". Her reply was perfect, "It's not just us. We have our own families to be part of".

Chapter 17

My Biological Father

So who was Nathan Mintz? Who is the man I had been relentlessly pursuing? As we saw earlier it is fairly easy to amass his basic biographical information. We know he was intelligent, professionally accomplished, married twice, and the father of four. But what was he really like?

Was he kind? Was he thoughtful? Was he funny? Was he introspective? Did he value family and friendships? What really animated him?

As with so much else in this journey, without first-hand experience and observation, it is hard to be certain what I actually know about the man who is my biological father. Documentary evidence can take us only so far. Knowing that I could only get at best second-hand information I set out to find out whatever I could about this man from those who knew him best.

The most direct evidence available would be from his wives and children. As part of my research, I knew that Nathan's first wife Dorothy had died a long time ago. But what about his second wife, Edith? She was much younger and might still be living. After some false leads trying to find out about her, I finally found her obituary that was dated October 22, 2017. This was just five months before I started my journey by swabbing my cheek for 23andMe. Close, but no direct help.

As far as my half-siblings are concerned, they steadfastly refuse to acknowledge my existence. To this date, I have never even received a "not interested" message let alone any insight into who our father was.

So I turned my attention to my cousins. Michael Levine and his daughter Beth Hammond didn't know Nathan. And neither did Dawn Bhat. That left David Levine, Bob Berkowitz, and of course Maimoona. I sought their permission to include their insights in this book and set out to interview them to see what I could learn.

As Nathan's niece and (other than his children) his closest living relative Maimoona was a treasure trove of information. She not only had clear memories of him but was also in possession of a fair amount of documentary evidence such as letters, photos, etc. Using all of this it is possible to start putting together a more detailed account of this man.

Like virtually every man of his generation, Nathan served in the armed forces during World War II. As a doctor, he was part of a medical corps that was critical to the war effort. At the end of the war, he was part of a medical team that went into concentration camps to see what had happened and, as much as the medical knowledge and capabilities of the time allowed, save the beaten, diseased and emaciated prisoners that they found. Maimoona shared with me a lengthy letter that Nathan had sent to her family after one of the most difficult rescue efforts. Reading it I was struck by his insight, his eloquence, and his humanity. He describes in detail what he found, what he was able to do for these poor souls, and just as importantly what he wasn't able to do.

Here is a brief excerpt from the letter that should give you a good sense of the larger account. This describes his experience when he got to the children's ward.

> Each room contained between four and six beds, and in most of them were lying two children with their heads at opposite ends of the bed. The medical term for the end stage of malnutrition in children is "merasmus" but that is not adequate to describe the pitiful state of many of these children whose gaunt and wasted frames, hollow cheeks and an apathy amounting almost to a torpor bore mute but eloquent testimony of their ordeal. The Major told us that blood plasma infused into their sternum and breastbone had been responsible for some return of strength to many of them, but there was one little four year old boy lying on his side with his eyes staring into space and breathing very faintly who was apparently beyond the reach of medical aid. I was told that all the mothers of these children had died, and had it not been for the advance of our armies I'm

certain that those still remaining would not have been long for this world

At the end of the letter Nathan sums up his feelings with:

Here again, as among the children, there was no external rejoicing at their liberation, nothing but apathy and listlessness and broken spirits which were more terrible to behold than outright grief. Those to whom I spoke, mainly Polish Jews, were quite matter of fact in their account and mentioned the loss of husbands, wives, brothers and sisters in almost a casual tone devoid of any emotion.

Even now, as I write, the whole experience seems too utterly fantastic and unreal to believe, and I know that I cannot convey to you even one iota of what I feel all that I had read before of the Nazi sadism has been amply confirmed and my hatred for them has become so intensified that it is almost something tangible.

As a Jew who was raised on the mantra "Never Again" I have often wondered how I would have dealt with situations like the ones Nathan found himself in. I do know that I often resort to humor or lightheartedness to get through tough times. I sometimes get myself into trouble because it can seem insensitive to make light of a horrible situation. All I know though is that it works for me. And as you can see in this picture, it looks like Nathan did the same.

Nathan Mintz freeing a German concentration camp

David Levine had more than a passing knowledge of Nathan. David's father Jules was Nathan's accountant and Nathan was his mom's OB/GYN. In fact cousin Nat delivered David and his brother at Doctor's Hospital. He told me that Nathan was loved by everyone. He recounted that Nathan had an impeccable reputation in the New York medical community.

As the interview was winding down he casually mentioned that I should speak to his mother. Until that mention, I had no idea that she was still alive. He offered to call her and ask if she would be interested in speaking with me. When I heard back that she was, I quickly set up a call with her.

Joan Levine was the quintessential Jewish mother. At 87 she was sharp of mind and sharp of tongue. Lots of strong opinions but also incredible compassion. We were on the phone for well over an hour. For the first twenty minutes or so she basically mothered me. She wanted to be sure that I was OK. She wanted to know how I was doing with this unnerving news. She assured me that regardless of what I learned or who I was able to make contact with that everything would be fine. With this kind of attention, it was no wonder that we easily established a wonderful rapport.

Though there were no online doctor reviews in those days, she told me that Nathan had been described more than once as the "finest OB/GYN at Mt. Sinai." She mentioned that Nathan had many famous clients and had even delivered the mayor's baby. From her vantage point, it seemed to the outside world as if Nathan had it all. She described him as handsome, bright, dignified, and refined. He was the 'golden boy' who was sought after for high society social events.

While Joan extolled Nathan's professional skills and achievements and could easily see how he was perceived by others, she also knew about the more difficult parts of his life. She went on at some length about the many travails he faced. This included in his medical practice, his two marriages, and even with his children.

She made it a point to say that there was quite a bit of discord in Nathan and Dorothy's marriage and that led to their divorce sometime in the mid to late 1950s. This was corroborated by Maimoona who told me that she too observed the tension in their relationship. Despite having three children together Joan thought that they just didn't like each other. In her view, they stayed in the marriage more out of convenience than love. Dorothy's money provided a very high-end lifestyle and Nathan's prestige opened doors throughout the upper echelons of New York society.

While there was universal agreement that Nathan was a brilliant man and an accomplished doctor it often takes much more than that to have a successful private medical practice. According to Joan part of Nathan's success in becoming a go-to Park Avenue OB/GYN was due to Dorothy. Dorothy Luria came from a very wealthy family in the steel and silver industries. Joan was convinced that her money and family connections were critical in getting Nathan's practice off the ground. As is often the case, people achieve success through a combination of personal traits such as skill, intelligence, grit, and hard work as well as the good fortune of coming from (or in this case marrying into) an influential family. Regardless of what the precise mix was with Nathan, there was no dispute that his practice flourished.

Joan thought that to some extent Nathan's professional success was at the expense of his children. She didn't observe him being particularly warm or nurturing with them. She thought that Max had a particularly difficult time with his father. If this is true, and if it persisted throughout his life, it is little wonder that Max had no interest in connecting with me.

After his divorce, Nathan married a much younger woman. Edith was 16 years younger than Nathan and she was or had been a patient of his. I have no information about how they became romantically involved and whether or not it crossed any ethical doctor/patient boundaries. Joan believes that Nathan's marriage to Edith was the beginning of a long slide downward for him. In her telling, Edith was intent on spending Nathan's money on lavish vacations and other extravagances.

In the middle of the picture below, you can see Nathan, with Edith partially on his lap, ready to depart on a Caribbean cruise. I don't know who the other visitors sitting down are. However, standing in the rear of the cabin is his teenage niece Myrna (now Maimoona).

Nathan and Edith Mintz setting sail, 1960

Looking at this picture I wondered if Nathan and I really had any physical resemblance. Recall, if you will that I am famously bad at this. Early in the search process, before I knew that Nathan was my father, I was rather fixated on the question of whether or not we looked like each other. Lots of people thought that the young adult Nathan and Joel bore a striking resemblance. What about as middle-aged men? I extracted middle age Nathan (age 48) from the cruise picture and found one of me from my 50th birthday party.

Now what do you think?

Joan told me that after his marriage to Edith, Nathan's practice started to decline. He reached the point where he had to give up his Park Avenue office and move in with another practice on 5th Avenue. This coincided with a change in his patient population. As Joan describes it, Nathan went from being the doctor of celebrities to dealing only with women from union households.

Nathan died in 2001 at the age of 89. Regardless of Joan's take on his marriage to Edith, it remained intact for over 40 years. This is way longer than his marriage to Dorothy. Edith's obituary in 2017 indicated a woman with some varied interests!

> Loving wife of Nathan. Devoted mother of Rachel. Dedicated companion to pets Cookie, Geary, Minna, Mignon, Boris and Zoe. Lover of transatlantic travel, French food, Mozart and English murder mysteries.

So we end where we began. Who was Nathan Mintz? Had I not stumbled into the interview with Joan I wouldn't have heard a negative word about him. Even considering her recollections from decades ago, we get a picture of a complex man who was without question extremely intelligent and accomplished.

According to Joan, there was no way she could see Nathan having an affair with my mom. If she is right, then that means I am one of Nathan's most notable professional accomplishments!

Chapter 18

What Really Happened?

Sometime during the week of June 21, 1948, my mom (and maybe my dad) headed from their apartment in the Bronx to the office of Dr. Nathan Mintz on Park Avenue in Manhattan. The weather that week was quite varied. Most days were in the upper 80's and humid. Typically hot for early summer in New York. But on one day it never managed to even reach the 70's. The old IRT rail cars were still in use and must have been quite hot for the 30-minute ride downtown. What was my mom thinking about and what was she expecting at the end of this ride? And then what exactly happened when she got there?

What we know for sure is that I was conceived in this time period from the sperm of Nathan Mintz. But exactly how had it happened? The short answer to that question is that we will never know for sure. Too much time has passed for any first-hand accounts to be available. And it is also extremely unlikely that there are any documentary records of what happened.

Just because any direct evidence is absent doesn't mean that we have no idea what might have happened. Understanding the people involved and the most common practices of the time can inform the speculation and guide us in figuring out what are the most and least likely possibilities.

Though there are many theoretical possibilities of what actually happened, we can divide them into two distinct categories: artificial insemination vs some form of a sexual encounter. Let's deal with the second one first.

My first thought on this subject was that there was no way that my conception was the result of my mother and Nathan Mintz having one or more sexual encounters. But my first thought when learning about my DNA results was that Debbie had a different father. So first thoughts might not be so reliable.

Though Nathan Mintz was a respected professional who is spoken of highly by those who know him we do know that his second wife had been a patient of his. So sometime, somewhere, somehow the bright line of doctor-patient separation might have been breached. People fall in love all the time and in many unusual circumstances. So this fact alone doesn't mean that Nathan was someone who regularly preyed upon or had lapses of judgment with his patients. But could this actually have happened with my mom?

Let's look at what we know and don't know. We know that my mom had been trying to have a child for over five years. And we know that she sought out a well-regarded OB/GYN to help her with this problem. So, on one hand, she was primed and highly motivated to go along with anything he might suggest. Or, for that matter, might have had a creative suggestion or two of her own! But was she willing to cross this line? She was extraordinarily prudish when it came to anything sexual. She wouldn't/couldn't talk about it. She was extremely uncomfortable around public displays of affection that had even the slightest sexual component to them. She looked askance at even the most minimally sexually suggestive clothing. I know it is a cliché that every child cannot imagine his or her parents having sex. But in the case of my mother, I still can't! I used to think that there was hard evidence that she had had sex at least three times in her life. But given how I might have been conceived I would without hesitation drop that estimate to two!

Beyond the nature of the people involved, it hits me that Dr. Mintz would have been most eager to find a 'professional' solution to my parents' infertility issues. Although there weren't really any specialists in this area in 1948, he had shown professional interest in the subject. So, I am going to assume that he was not sexually involved with an extremely prudish patient of his. In one way or another, it strikes me that my conception was part of an infertility treatment rather than a sexual encounter.

There is another piece of evidence to support this conclusion. Debbie was able to locate Ida Weitz, who was in a nursing home in Massachusetts. She was the sister of our Aunt Lilly. Aunt Lilly was married to my mom's older brother Roland. Lilly and Roland were trying to have a child at the same time as my parents. And just like my parents they too were not having any luck. According to Ida, my mom, who was eight months pregnant with me, approached Lilly and told her, "I have a doctor that can really help you get pregnant". Lilly responded that she was tired of doctors. She and Roland wound up adopting a baby boy just two months later. What is significant to me about this anecdote was that my mother proactively approached Lilly with the offer. This means that she credited her being able to get pregnant to whatever Dr. Mintz had done for her. I really doubt she would have done this if her pregnancy was the result of a sexual relationship she had had with him.

All told, how sure am I of this conclusion? If I was on a criminal jury where the required level of proof is 'beyond a reasonable doubt' I would vote 'not guilty'. But if I were on a civil jury where the required level of proof is the more lenient 'preponderance of the evidence' I would vote 'guilty as charged!'

So with this caveat in place let's look at what exactly the infertility treatment might have been.

The ability to reliably freeze sperm for later use was not possible until the 1950s. So we can rule out the more clinical seeming situation where a physically present but psychologically distant technician in a white coat strides into the exam room with a previously created sample for a routine seeming procedure. The sample would have to still be 'fresh' for it to be effective. But how long would that be?

Inside a woman's vagina sperm can live for up to five days. This is the thankfully best situation for their longevity. Outside the vagina, though it depends greatly on how they are cared for. If precise conditions of warmth and humidity are maintained this could be as long as a few hours. But in 1948 the knowledge of these parameters would very likely be quite limited. Without any attention to the conditions of its environment, the freshly ejaculated sperm would only survive for minutes not hours.

Even if we assume that Dr. Mintz would be as knowledgeable as anyone about the best practices known at that time, it is very likely that the ejaculation was very close in time to the insertion. It is fairly easy for me to imagine a doctor giving the signal to a donor in another room and then collecting the sample and inserting it with a syringe (not the 'turkey baster' of popular lore!). I have a much harder time imagining the doctor as a secret donor, however.

He would have to excuse himself from the exam room, do the deed, and almost immediately return for the insertion as if nothing of significance just happened. Just because I find this hard to imagine doesn't mean it didn't happen exactly like this, however. There are many reported cases of doctors doing just this. So I am inclined to think this is indeed what happened.

The bigger question is who, besides Dr. Mintz, knew what was going on. Let's start with my father. I have seen numerous pictures of my father with me as a newborn and a young baby. Despite the certain upheaval in his life that a new baby created, the joy on his face is palpable. I have seen movies of those days and his happiness and playfulness are evident in every one of them. There is even a movie of him proudly carrying me from the hospital to a waiting taxi to bring me home. All of this suggests that he was completely besotted with the idea of fatherhood and **his** little baby boy.

Dad bringing me home from Doctor's Hospital

To further bolster this idea we actually were able to get a contemporaneous account of the situation. My father's best friend from childhood was Georgie Rothkopf. He and Georgie were very close. They

111

were best men at each other's weddings and maintained a close relationship till the day my dad died. Amazingly Debbie was able to find Georgie in 2018 at a nursing home in Dallas. He was 97 years old but still quite lucid and clear in his memories. When informed of the situation with me, he told Debbie that my dad definitely did not know what happened. He said, "We told each other everything. If he knew, I would have known."

The proud parents with me July 1949 (age 4 months)

On top of all this, my dad was very forthcoming with me about aspects of his life. I find it very hard to imagine him keeping a secret this large until his death 40 years later.

What about my mom? This one is harder to figure out. It is almost certain she knew that something was happening. But what did she know? Let's look at the possibilities.

At one extreme Dr. Mintz told her everything and asked her permission to proceed. I really, really doubt this is what happened. In those days women were not often considered to be full-fledged decision-makers.....even about their own health. Doctors would routinely consult the husband for these decisions. And my mom was not particularly astute about anything 'scientific'. In addition to this, she was often quite incurious about the world around her. When confronted with a challenging issue or unpleasant reality, rather than problem solve a solution, she would sometimes say she simply didn't want to know.

Another possibility is that she knew she was getting a donor's sperm but was not informed that it was the doctor's. While this might be a bit easier to imagine I don't think this occurred either. Other than the hidden identity of the donor this scenario suffers from the same issues as the first one.

The next case involves the insertion of the semen using a syringe with what my parents were told were my father's sperm. My historical research indicates that this was just starting to happen during this time period. Of course, the actual semen was either a mixture of my dad's and the doctor's or just the doctor's. While this would make them think that my dad was indeed my dad, it would certainly have been a noteworthy event in their lives. And as noteworthy as it would have been, there was never any mention of it from either of them. And it would also fail the "Georgie Rothkopf" test. So while this is more likely than the first two cases I am inclined to believe that this too did not happen.

That leaves us with only one other possibility. The good doctor treated my mother without informing her of what exactly was going on. He could have described it as an injection to facilitate fertility, something to cleanse the vagina, or just some lubrication. Or, given how incurious my mother could be, he might not have told her much of anything about it. In this scenario, it is more likely than not that not only was my dad not aware of what was happening but he wasn't even present when it did happen. As you can tell, this is the scenario that I now believe is the most likely one.

Clearly, my assessment of the likelihood of these different possibilities is just conjecture on my part. I will never know what actually happened. And if I am right about the secretive approach then this was not only unusual for the day but utterly unethical. Even by the conventions of the day, some type of informed consent would have been the proper way to proceed.

To take this one step further, the AMA indicated at the time that if a doctor assisted a woman through artificial insemination it would be unethical for him to then deliver the baby. The thinking was that since he knew that a donor was used he would have to lie if he entered the name of the husband as the father on the birth certificate. They recommended that a doctor utilizing donor insemination pass the woman off to another doctor who had no knowledge of the means of conception for the actual delivery.

Nathan Mintz is not only my biological father but he delivered me and signed my birth certificate indicating that George Gottfried was my father.

One question I have often pondered is, "Am I the only one?" In addition to my four half-siblings that Nathan Mintz fathered with his two wives did he father any other children? Might I have another or a few other or many other half-siblings? A simple Google search shows numerous stories with headlines like, "Doctor Used His Sperm To Father Hundreds Of Babies." At first, I thought they were just different news outlets reporting about the same case. But there really are many different doctors involved in stories like this.

Shortly after I revealed my story to friends and relatives, a friend of one of my relatives came forward with a similar tale. In his case, he had never known who his biological dad was. So it wasn't the same shock that I had when his DNA test revealed newfound relatives. However, his 47 (and counting!) half-siblings were certainly unexpected and life-altering.

There are three possibilities as to the existence of other half-siblings. The first is that the situation with Nathan and my mom was a one-off occurrence. For whatever reason, he tried this just once and for whatever reason never tried it again. Though this is possible it doesn't strike me as likely.

Another possibility is he used donor sperm on many occasions but that I was the one and only time that due to some emergency he used his own. Perhaps a scheduling mishap or another donor-related problem. In this scenario, Dr. Mintz was an ethical fertility specialist who had a momentary lapse of judgment. Just like the first case this too is possible but I think unlikely. In this case, the doctor would have been informing his patients about the use of donor sperm. Given my belief that my parents didn't know I was the result of donor insemination, I tend to discount this possibility.

The final case is that there were some (perhaps many) other cases just like mine. This would be consistent with the recently displayed news headlines. However, there is no evidence of this. And by evidence, I mean DNA evidence. I am registered on the four major DNA sites as well as the public site GEDMatch. If there are any other half-siblings out there the one thing I know for sure is that they haven't had their DNA tested. The only half-sibling of mine who shows up on any site is Debbie. That makes me doubt this possibility. As I looked more carefully at the news stories I noticed that almost all of them were significantly more recent than mine. Perhaps I do have many additional half-siblings but that the prevalence of DNA testing of people in their 70's is infrequent enough that any cases like this just haven't shown up yet. And as time goes on and any possible half-siblings of mine grow older there is even less likelihood that they will.

It hits me that if you think that all three possible outcomes are unlikely it just means that you really have no idea what happened. And I guess that is and will likely remain the unfortunate reality.

Chapter 19

What Now?

In April of 2015, as part of a visit to my son Jamie in Berlin, I traveled to Krakow Poland. It came highly recommended to me by friends who had recently been there. With its cobblestone streets, scenic squares, and a huge castle that is straight out of a fairy tale, the city just oozes old-world charm. But the main purpose of this visit was not to take in the Krakow of today but rather to reconnect with my Jewish heritage by visiting some of the most noteworthy and horrific sites of the holocaust. In particular, I was planning on visiting the infamous Auschwitz concentration camp which is about 45 miles from the city. After careful research ahead of time I hired a guide for not only a tour of the camp but for a full-day tour of the area that included other equally chilling, if less well-known, sites and memories.

Jacob, my tour guide, was a PhD student specializing in the holocaust. For good measure, he was also an accomplished Jewish genealogist. There are few days in my life I remember as clearly as this one and that evoked such powerful emotions in me.

At Auschwitz, he not only gave me the full tour but provided the historical context of all I was seeing. At the very end of our visit, we went across the road to the Birkenau death camp. According to the Auschwitz museum:

> "Birkenau was the largest of the more than 40 camps and sub-camps that made up the Auschwitz complex....The majority—probably about 90%—of the victims of Auschwitz Concentration Camp died in Birkenau. This means approximately a million people. The majority, more than nine out of every ten, were Jews."

At Birkenau there was a rail spur where the boxcars crammed full of deported Jews would complete their journey. As the Jews were unloaded from the cars, those that were still alive would be placed on the cement train platform and sorted into groups of those capable of work from those who were unable to provide any useful services to the camp. Jacob told me that late in the war, well after the outcome was no longer in doubt, the Germans actually accelerated the rate at which the Jews were rounded up and transported there. In particular, Jews from Hungary were among the last to arrive. And given the frantic nature toward the war's end, they weren't even sorted. They were just basically marched from the rail spur directly to the crematoria just a few hundred yards away. The crematoria were in continuous operation incinerating people as fast as they could be loaded.

Under a clear April sun, Jacob and I made the same walk that the Hungarian Jews had made. I had actual chills up my spine, tears in my eyes and my body shuddered at the thought that we were taking the very same steps as those unfortunate people had a little more than 60 years earlier. Needless to say, there were many, many moving and horrific sites at the Auschwitz complex that I had seen that day. Some of them made me sad or wince at the thought of what had happened or even gasp in disbelief. But nothing came close to how I felt walking the same path as those Hungarian Jews who had just been extracted from the rail cars.

My dad's family was Hungarian and I felt an incredibly powerful connection with these people. I was absolutely certain that I was literally walking in the footsteps of some direct ancestors of mine. It was the most moving part of an unforgettable day.

Except I now know that these people were not actually my ancestors. George Gottfried's ancestors are Hungarian but mine are not. Besides my dad and my Grandma Gussie, I didn't know any of them and I wasn't related to them either. Nathan Mintz's family, my actual ancestors, came from Russia. So in some sense, what was the most personal and moving moment of the trip was based on misinformation and not really personal at all.

Despite this, I still feel a kinship with the plight of Hungarian Jews way more than I do for the Russian Jews who went through comparable (or worse) fates. I still wonder about the lives and stories of Hungarian immigrants to the US and not so much about Russian ones. I am still way more interested in stories of modern-day Hungary than modern-day Russia. I still harbor thoughts about taking that "roots" trip to Hungary with my sons, even though these are not actually our roots. The Hungarian part of me has been such an important part of my identity for so long that it has not been torn asunder by the identity of a few pesky genes! Even though it is a fact that my biological ancestors are from Russia my emotional ancestors are still from Hungary.

It has been an interesting exercise to think through why my Hungarian 'heritage' so strongly dominates my identity. Not only compared to my newfound Russian ancestry but also my mother's side of the family. Her family has both British and German roots. I know a good deal less about her side of the family than my dad's side. I don't think it was coincidental that I chose to pursue my dad's side when I began my genealogy research many years ago. I have just felt a closer kinship with them. Perhaps it was because I felt closer to my father than my mother.

On the other hand, the grandparent I was closest to was my mom's father, Grandpa Abe. He was born in the US, a rarity for New York Jews of that generation. I have many fond memories of him telling me stories, playing games, and just being present in my life in a way my other grandparents weren't or couldn't.

When I was a little boy, Grandpa Abe would regale me with fantastical adventure stories. In each one, the hero would get himself into seemingly impossible to escape situations. And just as I was wondering what would happen next, Grandpa would say of the hero: "He stepped on a piece of tin, and the tin bended and the story ended." And I would howl with laughter. For some reason, I never expected this even though every single story ended this way.

After his wife (Grandma Sadie) died, Grandpa Abe came to live with us for a while. He always wore a jacket and tie to dinner. In those days, much to my parents' chagrin, I had long hair, bell-bottom pants, and always sported a necklace of some sort. My mother in particular was convinced I was a degenerate hippie who was lacking in self-respect. One night at dinner, my grandfather asked me, "Why do you wear those beads?" I thought about it for a minute and replied, "It is just like you wearing a tie. It makes me feel complete." He thought about my reply for another minute and calmly said, "That makes sense," and went about eating his dinner. I thought my mother was going to keel over in disbelief.

Grandpa Abe lived to the ripe old age of 97 and was an ongoing presence in my life well into adulthood. Despite this, my interest in his side of the family did not extend much beyond him. I was instead endlessly interested in my dad's ancestry.

118

Four generations 1978. Grandpa Abe (age 96), mom, baby David and me

One year when I was visiting my grandparents' gravesites I looked more closely at Grandpa Jimmy's headstone. I knew that he had died just a few days after Debbie was born. When I looked more closely at his birth date I realized that he died when he was 67 years old. And, as it happened, my dad died when he too was 67. I made this realization when I was in my early 60's and then was haunted as to what might happen to me when I turned 67. Of course the year I reached that age came and went without any major incident (although I was diagnosed with multiple myeloma when I was 68). Of course, my concern for some genetic predisposition to dying in your 60's, while a stretch, to begin with, was completely non-existent. I now know that I don't share any genes with these two men. None. Perhaps I can take after the man whose genes I do share, Grandpa Abe. I promise that the year I turn 97 I won't obsess about my mortality!

Before every monthly visit to the oncology clinic to get my myeloma infusion I am asked to review all of my information. In addition to contact info and insurance numbers etc., they ask you to review your medical and family histories. Since this never changes I just click, 'Yes' when asked if it is accurate. Before one recent visit, I thought I would take a closer look. One of the entries indicated that I had a family history of diabetes. This is because my father had diabetes. But my dad's diabetes has absolutely nothing to do with me. So I asked to have it removed. I have been wondering how often people get to change their family history in their medical database.

By the way, I also noticed that there was an entry for hiccups as one of my medical conditions. Hiccups! I guess at some point I had a severe enough case to mention and have entered in my records. But I have no recollection of when or how this happened. I don't even recall when the last time I have ever hiccupped. So, for good measure, I asked them to remove this too. And to the best of my knowledge, neither George nor Nathan had a serious hiccup problem.

So where am I now?

There are days when I am consumed by thoughts and musings of what this all means to me. And there are days when I don't think about it at all.

There are days when I am mad at Nathan Mintz for tricking my parents. And there are days when, as Susan said, I thank him for my intelligence.

There are days when I am angry at my mother for either colluding with the doctor or willfully ignoring what happened. And there are days when I celebrate her determination to bring me to life.

There are days when I really miss the connection with my newfound siblings that has the potential to shed a whole new layer of understanding into who I am. And there are days when I just shrug it off and think it is their loss more than mine.

There are days when I wonder what life might have been like had George been my biological father. And there are days when I fully understand that he was my father and that this is a complete non-issue.

There are days when I wonder who I would be if I was in fact raised by the father who conceived me. And there are (many more) days that I am just happy being me.

I was recently asked by a close friend what my Covid learnings were. It was an intriguing question. For me, Covid followed shortly after my myeloma diagnosis and the surprising DNA results that upended my identity. Because of my age and especially my myeloma, I was, and despite being vaccinated, continue to be at significantly elevated risk of Covid. A year of severely limited activities and a reduced social life left a lot of time to ponder things in general and to repeatedly revisit the basic "Who am I?" question. My answer to her was not so much what I might have learned during Covid but just that I had become much more contemplative about who I am and life in general.

Another question that I get all the time is, "Knowing how this all turned out, would I do it all over again?" Or put more directly, "Am I glad that I unearthed this deeply buried secret about my identity?" These are very simple questions for me. My resounding answer to each is YES! To paraphrase a popular aphorism, "It is better to have known and been shocked than never to have known at all".

In some ways, as fundamental and existential an issue as the identity of my biological father is, it is in many ways not unlike the other huge issues that I have had to deal with in my life. In 2006 I had an undiagnosed case of endocarditis that only resolved itself with emergency open-heart surgery to replace my aortic valve. I came within a couple of days of death. Needless to say, this too engendered a great deal of self-reflection and asking the "Who am I?" question.

Although not immediately life-threatening, having an incurable form of cancer is another wake-up call to be sure that you center yourself, focus on what is important and repeatedly pose and re-answer that very same question, "Who am I?"

After going through the entire gambit of emotions surrounding my paternal ancestry I have come full circle. I now find it more rewarding and useful to ponder "Who am I?" than "Who's my daddy?"

As a hard-core atheist, I don't believe there is an afterlife. But that doesn't mean that who you are completely dies when your body finally gives way to its inevitable collapse. For me, eternity is all about memories. When you are alive you can connect with the past by nurturing the memories of your ancestors (hence my regular cemetery trips and my keen interest in genealogy). When you die, you get to leave behind memories of yourself with your family and loved ones who survive you. After my myeloma diagnosis and the more uncertain nature of what my remaining lifespan might be, I have given this a lot of thought. If I get to live long enough to help and see each of my three grandchildren grow into happy and productive young adults I will end my life fulfilled. Hopefully, I can leave them with memories of me that they can then nourish and carry forward to their own families.

Acknowledgments

When thinking about who I wanted to acknowledge, I wondered what it is I am acknowledging them for. Help with the book? Help with the search? Supporting me in my life?

Regardless of which of those areas merited acknowledgment my ~~half~~ sister Debbie is at the top of the list. A lifetime of love and support set the stage for her unflinchingly helping me figure out my family identity. Even though we don't share all of the biology we had always assumed, she is my full family in every sense of the word. I couldn't have taken this journey without her.

I would never have been able to find my biological father without the cooperation and openness of my newfound cousins. My deepest appreciation goes out to David Levine, Joan Levine, Michael Levine, Beth Levine Hammond, Dawn Bhat, Bob Berkowitz, and Maimoona Ahmed. Maimoona has been an invaluable lifeline to my new family and helps me stay connected.

Gene Dershewitz played a small but critical role in my search. Without his willingness to assist me, I never would have connected with Maimoona. And without Maimoona, there is no discovery. Thanks Gene!

When I was in complete denial about my shocking discovery, my cousin Roy came to the rescue. I am so thankful to him for his eagerness to help out with his DNA. This proved that the search was necessary.

Special thanks go to Georgie Rothkopf and Ida Weitz. They knew my parents well and were kind enough to provide important corroborating information. I want my memory to be as sharp as theirs when someone reaches out to me in 25 years!

This book would have looked very different without the help of my editor, Beth Rothschild. She helped me flesh out the story so that it provided a much more well-rounded account of who I am to accompany the search itself. And she undertook a personal 'comma-kazi' mission to ensure that this was all grammatically proper.

I really doubt that I would have succeeded in my search had I not been inspired by the work of Lennard Davis to seek out my mom's OB/GYN. When I contacted him to compare notes, he was very encouraging and even gave me some tips on writing this book.

I was alerted to Lennard Davis' story by my daughter-in-law Erin. This was possible only because she keeps my needs in the forefront of her thoughts more than a man can reasonably expect a daughter-in-law to do.

When I first told him I was thinking about writing this book, my son David, offered to design and construct the book cover. And as you can see he was wildly successful. This was just one way that he offered his love and support with this project and way beyond.

My son Jamie was always the perfect sounding board for my ideas and theories. He helped me hone my thinking and analyze the different options. He not only looks like me (so they say!) but thinks like me (only younger and quicker!).

My wife Susan was my rock throughout this process. Present at every step of the way. She not only lent her wordsmithing expertise when needed and provided an extra set of (quite beautiful) eyes to review the manuscript but also offered the love and comfort that kept me on an even keel whenever I started to wobble.